Indians of the Northwest Coast

INDIANS

OF THE

NORTHWEST COAST

by **PHILIP DRUCKER**

Bureau of American Ethnology

Smithsonian Institution

Anthropological Handbook **NUMBER TEN**

Published for

The American Museum of Natural History

McGraw-Hill Book Company, Inc.

New York   Toronto   London

INDIANS OF THE NORTHWEST COAST

Library of Congress Catalog Card Number: 55-9543

Published by the McGraw-Hill Book Company, Inc.
Printed in the United States of America

PREFACE

The AMERICAN MUSEUM OF Natural History has exceptionally fine collections from the Northwest Coast of America, particularly from the Indian groups of the northern half of that region, that is, from the coasts of British Columbia and southeast Alaska. A good part of this material was collected in the closing decades of the nineteenth century when the Indians preserved ancient patterns and standards of values to a considerable extent, and there were still many expert practitioners of the rich and distinguished aboriginal art. Portions of these collections were made in connection with expeditions sponsored by the American Museum of Natural History for the purpose of studying the colorful, vigorous native civilization of the area. The purpose of the present work is not, however, to present a catalogue of the collections, nor is it to serve as a simple guide to them in the ordinary sense. Its aim is to sketch in the cultural background of the specimens by relating briefly not only how the various material objects were made and used, but recounting something of the general way of life of the makers and users. It therefore discusses at some length a variety of aspects of culture that cannot of themselves be displayed in a museum case: social customs, religious beliefs, and ceremonial patterns. The aim is to make the specimens on exhibition more meaningful by describing the way in which they formed a part of the lives of the aboriginal people of the Northwest Coast.

Only fragments are to be found today of the aboriginal civilizations described in these pages. Many of the Indians of the coast are nowadays commercial fishermen and loggers. Most of them are more at home with gasoline and Diesel engines than with the canoes of their forefathers. Membership in one or another Christian church is universal. The ancient art style has very nearly disappeared. Men no longer have time to carve and paint when they have to make a living in the competitive modern society. Here and there a few relics of ancient patterns have been preserved more or less deliberately. Some groups occasionally still give festivals and feasts in the ancient potlatch tradition; others retain certain of the ancient social forms, such as the clan organization. A few Chilkat Tlingit women weave the traditional type of robe. Among other groups the women still make basketry or cedarbark mats. But aside from these fragments and the people's pride in their identity as Indians, Northwest Coast culture must be regarded as having disappeared, engulfed by that of the modern United States and Canada.

Philip Drucker

CONTENTS

ILLUSTRATIONS

Indians of the Northwest Coast

ONE

INTRODUCTION

THE LAND

Along the shores of northwestern North America from Yakutat Bay
in southeast Alaska to Trinidad Bay on the coast of present northern
California, lived a number of Indian groups who participated jointly in a
unique and rich culture. It is an anthropological truism that development
of complex, or "high," culture among primitive peoples is linked with,
or, better, results from the notable increase in economic productivity
that accompanies the invention or acquisition of agricultural techniques, and within limits, the domestication of animals. This can be
documented by archaeological evidence from various early centers
of high civilization—the Middle East, the Indus Valley, Middle
America. The expansion of the economic base effected by agriculture
raises the general standard of living, permits increased settled popula-
tions, provides more leisure time to cultivate the arts, to elaborate on
religious, social, and political concepts, and to perfect the material
aspects of culture: tools, dwellings, utensils, textiles, ornaments, and
the rest. The culture of the Northwest Coast, therefore, seems to be
an anomaly, for it was a civilization of the so-called "hunting-and-
gathering" type, without agriculture (except for a few instances of
tobacco growing), and possessing no domesticated animals other
than the dog. In other words, the natives of the Northwest Coast, like
the rude Paiute of Nevada, the Australian aborigines, and others of

I

the simpler cultures the world over, were entirely and directly dependent on natural products for their livelihood. That they were able to attain their high level of civilization is due largely to the amazing wealth of the natural resources of their area. From the sea and rivers, fish—five species of Pacific salmon, halibut, cod, herring, smelt, and the famous olachen or "candlefish" (this last so rich in oil that a dried one with a wick threaded through it burns like a candle), and other species too numerous to mention—could be taken in abundance. Some of these fish appeared only seasonally, but were easy to preserve. The sea also provided a tremendous quantity of edible mollusks; "when the tide goes out the table is set," as the saying goes. More spectacular was the marine game: hair seal, sea lion, sea otter, porpoise, and even whale. On shore, land game too abounded. Vegetable foods were less plentiful, although many species of wild berries were abundant in their season. In other words, the bounty of nature provided that which in most other parts of the world man must supply for himself through agriculture and stock raising: a surplus of foodstuffs so great that even a dense population had an abundance of leisure to devote to the improvement and elaboration of its cultural heritage.

The Northwest Coast is a unit, not only in its aboriginal culture patterns, but geographically as well. The Japanese Current offshore moderates the climate so that extreme and prolonged cold does not occur even in the higher latitudes. The same ocean stream releases vast amounts of water vapor that is blown onshore by the prevailing winds, condenses on rising over the coastal mountains and hills, and produces the characteristic heavy rainfall of the area. Consequently, innumerable streams and small rivers with their sources in the Coast Range flow to the sea, as do the major drainage systems like the Columbia, the Fraser, and the Skeena, with sources east of the mountains. Likewise, the heavy precipitation produces a dense specialized vegetation, consisting mainly of thick stands of conifers—Douglas fir, various spruces, red cedar, yellow cedar, yew, and, at the southern tip of the area, coast redwood. Deciduous trees are smaller and more scattered, but include several hardwoods, such as maple and oak, and the soft but even-grained alder.

The terrain is of two major types, which grade into each other in the Gulf of Georgia–Puget Sound region. In the north, the Coast Range is composed of towering mountains of raw, naked rock. Deep cañons, gouged out by glacial flow and turbulent streams, cut into them. A general subsidence in ancient geological times has "drowned" many of these valleys and cañons, producing long narrow fiords flanked by sheer cliffs rising hundreds of feet. The scenery is spectacular; travel, except by water and over a few rare passes, is painful and slow. As one goes southward the terrain changes until, around upper Puget Sound and the Oregon and northwestern Californian coasts, one sees steep but rounded coast hills, not mountains; estuaries resulting from the building up of sand bars form at river mouths, indicating the gentler gradients of the lower portions of the stream beds.

The areal fauna, like everything else, is highly specialized. Varieties and abundance of marine forms have been mentioned. The principal large game animals were deer, elk, and, on the mainland from the Gulf of Georgia northward, mountain goats. Where long northern fiords cut entirely or partially through the Coast Range, hunters had access to subarctic faunal assemblages, including caribou and moose. Coastal carnivores included chiefly wolf, black and grizzly bear, and brown bear in the north, mountain lion, and a variety of small fur bearers: beaver, mink, marten, and land otter, among others. A number of intriguing problems related to the distributions of land species, especially in the island areas along the Inland Passage, though they have little connection with areal culture patterns, are of passing interest. For example, on the Queen Charlotte Islands there were black bear and a type of small caribou, but no grizzly bear or deer. (The modern deer population has descended from a few pairs imported by white settlers some forty or fifty years ago.) On Vancouver Island deer, elk, wolf, mountain lion, and black bear, among the larger forms, occurred, but neither mountain goat nor grizzly. A small "black bear" with an all-white coat, known as Kermode's bear, was found in the vicinity of Princess Royal Island, and apparently nowhere else. Up the coast, nearly every major island from Admiralty Island north seems to have its own distinctive subspecies of Alaskan brown bear. It is possible that the deer population of northwestern California tended to show much greater color variation than in other areas. To return from oddities of distributions to the general faunal picture, the Pacific flyway follows the coast for a great part of its length, and enormous flights of waterfowl of many species flew along it on their annual migrational round.

Few modern students of human society will subscribe to a theory of environmental determinism of culture. Yet, while the geographical background of aboriginal Northwest Coast civilization can by no means be said to have defined the culture patterns of the area, it can be shown to have had a certain influence, by permitting, and even inducing, development along some lines, and inhibiting that along others. Some of the environmentally affected cultural elaborations are included among the patterns that make the areal culture as a whole distinctive, as compared with other native civilizations of North America. It is true enough that in other equally important area-wide patterns no environmental factors can be detected, but those in which the physical setting played a part are worth discussing.

Marine resources may be considered first. We have seen that they were tremendously rich, and in addition, partly seasonal (that is, the "runs" of certain important species of fish, such as salmon, herring, smelt, and olachen, occur for a limited period each year). The abundance of these resources made a relatively dense population possible, once techniques had been devised to exploit them properly. Even more basically, it favored the orientation of the areal culture toward the water—the river and sea—with a consequent interest in development of water transport, that is, development of vessel construction and navigation. In fact, in the northern, more rugged half of the area it seems probable that a certain minimum proficiency in canoemanship must have been essential to the earliest human occupancy; it is difficult to see how people could have survived without it. At the same time, it is possible to interpret the richness of the fisheries resource as a limiting factor also: concentrated, as the "runs" of salmon and the other fish were, at the upper ends of bays and channels, or along the beaches, they may have restricted interest in water transport to the foreshore. It is certain that the Indians of the Northwest Coast were not deep-sea navigators in the same sense as the Vikings or the Polynesians. They sailed along the coast, from point to point, and hated to get out of sight of land.

Another feature of the natural environment that affected culture growth was the seasonal aspect of the principal "harvests" of fish. This made for periods of intense activity, put a premium on the development of techniques for the preservation of foodstuffs, and, once such techniques had been developed, permitted lengthy periods of leisure. In fact, once adequate preservation techniques had been developed, not only was there opportunity for leisure, but there was a certain force for seasonal immobility; even a large family group is unlikely to favor a nomadic way of life if they have half a ton of dried salmon to lug around with them. This leisure and temporary immobility was utilized by the Indians of our area for the development of art and ceremonialism. Here of course is where the strictly environmental interpretations of culture break down. The particular fields of interest that were seized on were determined by historical and social factors of human culture, and not by environment at all. All the environment did was to make possible the development of economic techniques that permitted considerable leisure. How that leisure was utilized was not defined by the natural setting—as far as environmental forces were concerned it might as well have been spent at studies of mathematics or crossword puzzles. The important thing is that the natural resources were such that they permitted the expansion of some luxury aspects of culture.

Another environmentally favored development was that of woodworking. As will be brought out, there were undoubtedly historical factors involved in the original interest in this activity, but the fact that the forests of the Northwest Coast were amply supplied with an abundance of readily worked woods made elaboration of this craft possible, and even might be said to have offered a certain inducement to such elaboration. Wood was beyond all question the most abundant type of material available. Moreover, other materials suitable for technological developments were scarce.

Some inhibiting factors of the environment may be pointed out. In the northern half of the area, unquestionably because of the roughness of the terrain, land hunting was a luxury activity, not a major field of economic endeavor. Another example: the mountainous northern coasts were formed of massive blocks of tough igneous rocks; work in stone was of minor importance throughout the area as a consequence, since stone that lent itself to working was relatively rare. There are exceptions. A very tractable form of slate occurs at a few localities in the Queen Charlotte Islands, but given the general absence of a stoneworking pattern, little or no use was made of it until historic times brought new cultural stimuli. Again, the northern half of the area has little land suitable for agriculture. Agriculture is a very minor form of economy today. Even if, in aboriginal times, contacts with agricultural areas had made possible the introduction of the art (as far as we know, there were no such direct contacts), it could never have had much effect on native culture, at least in the north. Even though there was a much-disputed plant—a tobacco or one resembling tobacco—supposed to have been cultivated in the Queen Charlotte Islands, and a true native tobacco was planted and harvested along the lower Klamath River in modern California, agriculture could never have reached a point where it would have modified the prevailing fishing and sea-hunting economy of the coast.

We may summarize our survey of the natural setting as follows: There were certain permissive factors in the environment that allowed cultural developments in certain aspects of native culture. Some of these—dependence on exploitation of marine resources, elaboration of canoe navigation, emphasis on woodworking—came to be distinctive of the areal culture. Some negative characteristics of the area, such as minor importance of land hunting, very rudimentary development of stoneworking, and the like, are due to inhibiting factors of the natural scene which did not provide adequate materials. However, many other features of coastal culture that served to mark it off as different from most other Indian civilizations of North America can be traced only to historical factors, or to the selection of certain solutions to problems posed by functional relationships of strictly cultural, not environmental, phenomena.

THE PEOPLE

Along this rugged but bountiful coast lived a number of Indian nations who differed among themselves somewhat in physical characteristics, differed considerably in language, but shared a number of fundamental cultural patterns that, in combination, comprised Northwest Coast civilization. It must be noted that here, as elsewhere throughout this book, the term "nation" is used with certain reservations, for as will be explained below, there were no nations in the modern political sense. There *were* groups, however, who spoke the same language or dialect of that language, who resembled each other more closely in details of culture than they did their neighbors of alien speech, and who consisted of independent local groups, tribes, or even confederacies, but who were without any sort of over-all "national" political authority or even sense of political unity.

Beginning our enumeration of Northwest Coast peoples in the north (map, Fig. 1), the Tlingit, consisting of fourteen tribal divisions, occupied the coast from Yakutat Bay to Cape Fox. They spoke a language believed by most linguists to be related to the Athapascan stock of the interior. Shortly before the opening of the historic pe-

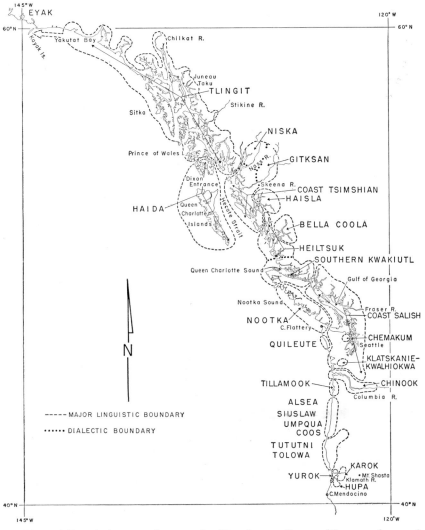

1. Map of linguistic groupings on the Northwest Coast. All names lettered in capitals refer to linguistic divisions; geographic names are lettered in lower case.

riod they were pressing westward. Some of their divisions, probably the Yakutat, had driven the Chugachmiut Eskimo off Kayak Island, and the same or some related tribe established an outpost among the linguistically (distantly) related Eyak of the mouth of the Copper River. A small Tlingit-speaking group, the Tagish, on Tagish and Marsh lakes (inland from the Chilkat Tlingit), possessed a culture of completely interior, not coastal, pattern, and were apparently an Athapascan people who were in the process of becoming Tlingit-ized through aboriginal trade contacts. According to tradition, the ancestors of some of the Tlingit clans once lived to the south, around the mouth of the Skeena, and subsequently moved northward. Other ancestral divisions migrated from the interior, following the Stikine River to the sea. If the traditions are to be believed, they reached salt water only after a perilous journey under a glacier that bridged a section of the river.

The Haida, who also spoke a language believed to be related to Athapascan, although differing from Tlingit, inhabited the Queen Charlotte Islands, and the southern part of Prince of Wales Island in Alaska. It is said that the Alaskan Haida, known as the Kaigani, drove out some Southern Tlingit tribe or tribes a little more than two centuries ago. There are two principal dialectic divisions among the Haida. These are called "Masset" and "Skidegate" after two important centers where the speakers of each assembled during historic times, following the sharp decline of the population. Most if not all the Kaigani came from the northern or Masset-speaking villages. Haida traditions relate that some of their ancestors—those belonging to the Eagle phratry (of which more later)—came from the mainland, but claim that the other Haida, whom the newcomers found living on the islands, had been there since the creation of the world.

The Tsimshian nation lived on the mainland and the adjacent islands. Each of the three major subdivisions spoke a slightly divergent dialect, and differed somewhat culturally. The first were the Niska, or Nass River tribes. The second, the Coast Tsimshian, consisted of fourteen tribes who held salmon-fishing villages on the lower Skeena River, and olachen-fishing grounds on the lower Nass. Nine of these tribes had separate winter villages along Metlakatla Pass, just off the modern city of Prince Rupert, and three had winter villages, one off the mouth of the Skeena, the other two to the south.

Two Coast Tsimshian tribes, the Kitselas and Kitsamxelam, wintered in their villages just below the cañon of the Skeena. The third major division, the Gitksan, inhabited eight villages above the cañon.

Some linguists classify the Tsimshian language with a proposed linguistic stock, as yet not certainly defined, for which they suggest the name "Penutian." The nearest fellow speakers of this stock were to be found far to the south, within the limits of modern Washington, Oregon, and California. According to Tsimshian tradition, most of their divisions came originally from a legendary place called Temlaxam ("Tum-la-ham"), "Prairie Town," located somewhere far up the Skeena. We are on surer ground when we consider more recent events: after the Hudson's Bay Company built Fort Simpson in 1834, the nine tribes who wintered on Metlakatla Pass shifted their winter quarters to Fort Simpson. In 1887 a large group, mainly from Fort Simpson, who were followers of the energetic missionary William Duncan, moved to a site on Annette Island, Alaska, where their descendants still live.

South of the Tsimshian were the Kwakiutl, with three major dialectic divisions: that spoken by the Haisla of Gardner and Douglas channels in the north, a second dialect called Heiltsuk, and Southern Kwakiutl. The Heiltsuk-speakers consisted of the Xaihais, the Bella Bella of Milbanke Sound, a historic confederation of several formerly independent tribes and local groups, and the Wikeno of Rivers Inlet. The traditional origin tales of all these people claim Rivers Inlet and lower Burke and Dean channels as their original homeland. The Haisla, for example, maintain that their ancestors came overland from Rivers Inlet. After settling at the old site of Kitamat, they incorporated a wandering Tsimshian clan. It is interesting to note that the names of their principal villages, "Kitamat" and "Kitlope," are Tsimshian, not Heiltsuk words; a possible interpretation is that their ancestors infiltrated a Tsimshian area and engulfed the former occupants (contradicting the traditional claim that the Haisla were there first). The Xaihais consisted of a number of independent local groups who, as a result of their lack of political unity, were being ground to bits between the warlike Coast Tsimshian and their own equally warlike Bella Bella relatives. The Bella Bella tribes seem to have held their own against all comers. Their drastic historic decline in population was effected by disease, rather than enemy successes. The present Wikeno represent a historic amalgamation of the original Wikeno of the Inlet, with the remnants of two tribes: the Nohuntsitk and the Somehulitk, of the upper and lower ends of Wikeno Lake, respectively.

The Bella Coola villages were located in the upper reaches of Dean and Burke channels and the lower parts of the Bella Coola River valley. These people spoke a Salishan language, fairly closely allied to the speech of the Coast Salish to the south, from whom they were separated by a considerable distance. Bella Coola traditions assert that this nation was created at the beginning of the world in the same locality (which we have just defined) where Alexander Mackenzie found them in 1793. However, in view of their linguistic affiliations, it seems more probable that their ancestors split off from the main body of Salish and migrated to their northern location. Various aspects of Bella Coola culture suggest either that they have been exposed to Heiltsuk influences a relatively short time or, more likely, that they were remarkably conservative in certain culture traits. Their material culture, their ceremonials, and their mythology check almost point for point with those of their Heiltsuk neighbors. In the field of social organization, however, particularly with respect to rank and social status, they have apparently retained to a great extent the amorphous, loosely organized Salish patterns rather than the precisely and rigidly defined ones of their neighbors.

The Southern Kwakiutl consisted of a large number of independent local groups and tribes occupying the bays and inlets around Queen Charlotte Sound and the entire northern end of Vancouver Island, as far south as Cape Cook. Like the Bella Coola, they insist that their ancestors were created in the region they now occupy; the possibilities are that they have occupied it for a considerable length of time. There is little evidence of any major population shifts among them, other than the expansion of the southernmost tribe, the Lekwiltok, into the Cape Mudge area at the expense of the Salishan Comox, and the separation of the Matilpe from the Fort Rupert confederacy. The Lekwiltok deserve special mention as one of the most warlike groups of the entire coast. Their original territory dominated Yucluta Rapids and Seymour Narrows, passes between Vancouver Island and the mainland. They exacted tribute or attacked anyone who traveled these roads, whether the party was a peaceful one going on a trading expedition or to a potlatch, or whether it was a Haida war party bent on slave raiding in Puget Sound. They were, of course, frequently attacked in retaliation, but always gave a good account of themselves.

On the southwest coast of Vancouver Island, or as it is locally known, the "West Coast," and on Cape Flattery, the extreme tip of the present state of Washington, live the Nootka. The Nootka language is distantly related to Kwakiutl; in fact, linguists consider that the two represent a single stock termed the Wakashan. It has been suggested that this stock, together with Salish and some other languages of the interior, may ultimately be related to Algonkian, a relationship that has not yet been demonstrated. There were two, or possibly three, dialectic divisions of Nootka—Nootka proper, spoken by the people from Cape Cook down to Barkley Sound—and Nitinat-Makah. It has not been established as yet whether Nitinat and Makah were minor variants of a single dialect, or whether they warrant separation into two distinct dialects. The Nootka possessed a specialized form of Northwest Coast culture—one extremely well adapted to the region. Only they (aside from a few neighbors of the Makah who learned the art from that last-named division) hunted the largest game on the coast—whales. Their basic canoe pattern was widely copied, and Nootka-made canoes were bought with eagerness by most of their neighbors because of their excellent lines and seaworthiness. The only territorial changes known to us from historical records or traditions are internal ones in which one Nootka local group or tribe exterminated or dispossessed another in order to acquire the victims' territories.

The land of the Coast Salish, aside from that of the Bella Coola, included the circumference of the Gulf of Georgia, Puget Sound, a good portion of the Olympic Peninsula, and most of western Washington, down to Chinook territory at the mouth of the Columbia River. One Salishan group, the Tillamook, resided south of the Columbia on the Oregon coast. As the name indicates, these Salish-speaking people were part of a larger linguistic entity, the bulk of whom lived in the interior to the east of the Cascades. This coast versus inland division appears to have been correlated with a major dialectic break, as well as with a differentiation between cultures of coast and inland genre. Great diversities of minor dialectic variants are recognized among the Coast Salish—the inhabitants of almost every drainage system, or at most, two or three contiguous valleys, had their own subdialects. There was a certain amount of intercourse between these coast people and their interior relatives. It is generally assumed that the coast divisions were relatively late entrants into the area, pushing down the Fraser River and spilling over the Cascades into western Washington. Such scant archaeological evidence as is available corroborates this theory, although the length of time the Salish have lived along the coast is not yet known.

A number of small enclaves of linguistically diverse groups occupied western Washington. On either side of the Nootkan Makah on the tip of Cape Flattery lived small divisions—the Chemakum on the Straits, and the Quileute on the Pacific Coast. Both of these spoke closely related languages, or dialects of the same tongue, but one not closely related to any other native North American language, although some authorities suggest a distant affiliation to a proposed group that includes Salishan, Wakashan, and Algonkian. The Chemakum became extinct too early for us to salvage any significant amount of linguistic or cultural data. We know that the Quileute borrowed heavily on the cultural side from their Makah neighbors, so that in historic times they varied from the Makah only slightly. A now extinct group, the Klatskanie, is reported to have held a sizable tract of territory in the midst of the Salish Chehalis. We know virtually nothing of this group, except that they spoke an Athapascan tongue. Presumably, they were culturally fairly similar to their Salish and Chinook neighbors. They were reputed to have been very warlike. Some time during the early historic period, they are reported to have moved from their territory on the Chehalis River across the Columbia to take up residence on the Clatskanie River in present Oregon. Another small Athapascan-speaking enclave, the Kwalhiokwa, about whom even less is known, held a tract along the Willapa River. One wonders if they may not have been a subdivision of the Klatskanie.

Along the lower Columbia, from The Dalles down to the sea, lived the various divisions of the Chinook. The exact relationship of their language to any other is unknown, although affiliation with the proposed widespread Penutian stock has been suggested. The great fame of the Chinook nation stems from the fact that they were middlemen in aboriginal trade north and south along the coast and between the coast and the interior. They traded slaves from the Californian hinterland up the coast for Nootka canoes and the prized dentalium shells, and exchanged many other products as well. It was through their hands that the strings of dentalia from the west coast of Vancouver Island eventually reached the Plains tribes east of the Rockies.

The central coast of Oregon, south of Tillamook territory, was occupied by several small groups now virtually extinct—the Alsea, the Siuslaw, the Coos, and the Umpqua. Very little information is available on these tiny divisions. Such as there is has been collected from informants who lived their lives in the cultural hodgepodge of Siletz and Grande Ronde reservations, on which all the Indians of western Oregon were assembled and thrown into intimate contact in the 1850s. Culturally these small tribes seem to have stood midway between the Salish-Chinook patterns and those of northwestern California; if anything, they inclined slightly more toward the former.

Another segment of the Athapascan linguistic family lived in southwestern Oregon. Villages of these people, who were sometimes referred to as the Tolowa-Tututni, after two of the better-known divisions, were situated along every stream course from the upper Umpqua to Smith River in northern California. These groups were culturally marginal to—that is to say, in many respects pallid imitations of—the civilization of the lower Klamath River. In this last-named region, representatives of three linguistic stocks—the Yurok of proven Algonkian affiliation, the Hupa of the Athapascan family, and the Karok of uncertain relationship—shared a set of cultural patterns modified from the basic motifs of the Northwest Coast and elaborated in a number of unique ways. Their civilization, simple and poor as it may seem in comparison with that of the northern tribes, was complex indeed as compared with that of their Oregon coastal neighbors and most of the native groups of California.

These, then, were the Indian nations participating in the unique patterns of the civilization of the Northwest Coast. Each group's manifestations of the fundamental motifs of areal culture differed a bit. All were not of the same intensity. Some groups were obviously borrowers, not elaborators, of ideas. Some may even have been "Johnny-come-latelies" to the coastal scene. Yet all shared and utilized a series of concepts that, like the weft strands in weaving, connect the various elements—in this context the local cultural variants—into a unit distinctive and unique among native American cultures.

PREHISTORY

The prehistory of the Northwest Coast, from which we may hope to learn the sources and development of the areal culture, has received relatively little attention up to this time. Excavations carried out around the turn of the century at sites along the lower Fraser River and on southeastern Vancouver Island indicated that there were at least two or three distinct cultural horizons there. The lower and older horizon was associated with skeletal remains of a longheaded population, quite different from the recent and historic Coast Salish. The latest level contained human remains of a broadheaded type, that resembled both the modern Coast Salish and the Interior Salish. This situation corroborates the assumption, based on linguistic and cultural grounds, that the Coast Salish were, relatively speaking, newcomers on the coast, having pushed their way out from the interior. These early researches did not succeed in defining any cultural differences associated with the population change. However, current studies in this region and in lower Puget Sound indicate that several marked cultural changes occurred and can be defined by use of precise modern archaeological techniques. Interestingly, the earliest horizon found appears to represent a culture oriented toward the sea and the utilization of marine resources, particularly the hunting of sea mammals. Considerable use was made of one-piece toggling harpoon heads of forms surprisingly like basic Eskimo patterns, used on bone foreshafts, and points and knives of ground slate. Heavy woodworking tools are absent on this early level, suggesting to one investigator that some sort of light composite water craft—possibly even skin-covered kayaklike vessels—may have been used. This early pattern was succeeded by others in which interior culture traits became more prominent, and the dominantly maritime aspect of the earliest culture was lost.

To the northward, only one extensive survey has been made. It produced no definitive results as to culture growth, but did demonstrate that archaeological sites are numerous, large, and deep, indicating a fairly lengthy occupation by people whose economy and material culture (particularly the canoe navigation complex) were oriented very much as were those of the Indians of early historic times. Since many of these sites can be identified by modern Indians and from early historical accounts as well, they offer an excellent opportunity to take advantage of the direct historical approach, working back from known identifiable cultures to the more ancient ones.

Somewhat more archaeological work has been done along the Columbia and the coast to the south. An investigation of the Dalles-Deschutes region indicates either that the Upper Chinook adopted patterns derived from the coast in relatively late times, or that they pushed upriver, driving out a group or groups whose culture was essentially of interior type.

At the extreme south of the area, on Trinidad Bay, a sequence of three horizons has been found so far: the uppermost, dating from historic times, is preceded by a late prehistoric period, and the latter by an early prehistoric stratum. At this writing full information is not available as to whether the two lower levels represent a developmental sequence or the replacement of one culture by a completely different one.

With the still scant amount of concrete evidence supplied by the archaeologist's shovel, trowel, and brush, it is useless to speculate at length on prehistoric sequences and developments. However, it may be pointed out that while it might have been theoretically possible for interior peoples gradually to have worked their way downstream to become the first human inhabitants of the northern California, Oregon, and Washington littorals, and of the Puget Sound–lower Fraser region, the first occupants of the rugged rockbound coasts to the north must, in all likelihood, have arrived with a sizable inventory of culture traits adapted to coast life: adequate canoe navigation, with all the appurtenances, knowledge, and skills for navigating those rough waters; tools and techniques for marine fishing and hunting and the like, if they were to survive. In other words, the sea-hunting early culture recently identified in the lower Fraser region may have been the basic pattern for the entire coast. Later entrants might, and no doubt did, come from the interior, and were able to exploit the coastal resources by adopting the implements and techniques of the original population. It is to be hoped that eventually enough careful scientific work may be done throughout the area to clarify the problems of the origins and growth of its unique culture.

PHYSICAL ANTHROPOLOGY *

From the land of the Tlingit south to the Fraser River, or possibly to the Puget Sound–Olympic Peninsula region, the Indians shared, and still share, certain similarities of appearance. They tend to range from tall to medium stature, with group means from about 5 feet 8 inches, in the north, to 5 feet 3 inches (173 to 162 centimeters), and are rather "stocky" in body conformation, with broad muscular chests and shoulders. As a rule they have broad heads (that is, heads which are wide in relation to length) and broad faces. An especially noteworthy characteristic is lightness of skin color. Unexposed (that is, un-sunburned) areas of the body are scarcely distinguishable in shade from the skin of many brunet Europeans. This is definitely not a result of race mixture during historic times; many of the early European explorers, like Captain Cook and Captain Vancouver, were struck by this fact, and made particular note of it in their descriptions of the people of the northern coasts. Hair tends to be coarse in texture, varies from straight to slightly wavy, and although popularly referred to as "black," is actually very dark brown. Men appear to have more profuse facial hair (mustaches and beards) than do other North American Indians. Well-developed "folds" at the inner sides of the upper eyelids are common.

Within this generalized physical type, there are several variations, some of which tend to mark off regional sub-types, and others that suggest results of mixture of distinct Indian types. The picture is complicated by the fact that the variant traits do not all correlate regionally. Stature, for example, shows an almost regular decrease from north to south, between south Alaska and the Fraser Delta. The Tlingit, when measured around the turn of the century, were tall people—the tallest on the coast—averaging 173 centimeters (5 feet 8 inches) in height. The Haida and Coast Tsimshian were still to be regarded as tall, averaging 169 centimeters; the Niska were a trifle shorter: 167 centimeters. To the southward, the series runs in the "medium" range: Bella Coola, 166 centimeters; Southern Kwakiutl, 164; Coast Salish of the Fraser Delta, 162. The Puget Sound Salish alter this trend by averaging 165 centimeters. Boas, who pioneered the investigation of the physical anthropology of the area as

* The data for this section were assembled from various published sources by Dr. Marshall T. Newman, Division of Physical Anthropology, U.S. National Museum.

well as those in linguistics and ethnography, interpreted this north-south stature trend as the result of gradual permeation of tall northern people, possibly originally Athapascans of the interior, southward along the coast, modifying an older short-statured population.

In addition to the stature gradient, Boas distinguished three regional sub-types on the British Columbia coast. He described them as follows:

"Northern sub-type" [Haida, Tsimshian]: This sub-type is characterized by tall stature, with relatively long arms, short trunks and long legs. The head is both very large and relatively broad, and the face is correspondingly quite broad, and only moderately long. The nose tends to be low, concave in profile, with a low root and broad alae. The Tlingit probably fit in this sub-type, their principal deviation being that of their greater average stature.

"Kwakiutl sub-type" [Kwakiutl and Bella Coola]: Medium rather than tall stature marks this group off from the preceding. In addition, bodily proportions differ considerably, the trunk being much longer in relation to length of limbs. Chests and shoulders are commonly very broad. The dimensions of the head are about like those of the northern sub-type. Facial proportions differ sharply, however; faces are not only very broad, but they are also relatively and absolutely extremely long. Lower jaws are massive and wide. The nose form typical of this subdivision is very long, relatively narrow, and highly arched, with a convex profile rarely seen in the north.

There are virtually no data on Nootkan anthropometry, but casual observation suggests that they conform to this physical pattern, except that high convex noses, and low-bridged concave ones, seem to be about equally common among them.

"Thompson River sub-type" [Coast and Interior Salish]: Boas found no objective means of distinguishing between the physical type of the Salish of the coasts and that of their relatives of the interior. In stature they are medium, ranging to the lower boundary of that category (165 to 162 centimeters). They also are broadheaded, but their heads are smaller in actual measurement, in both length and breadth, than those of their neighbors to the north. Their faces are broad, and proportionately and in actual measurement much shorter than those of the Kwakiutl. Noses are heavy, convex in profile, with a heavy long tip. The Salish also all tend to be slightly darker in skin color than the northerners.

One interesting feature of this survey is the thorough modification of the Bella Coola, who presumably once conformed to the physical sub-type of their Salish kinsmen. This fact suggests that not only were their closest contacts and intermarriages with the Kwakiutl, but that they may have maintained such contacts over a respectably long time period.

Such few archaeological data as are available indicate that the situation was not static. In the lower Fraser region, at least, there is definite evidence that an earlier population of different physical type, with relatively long narrow heads and narrow faces, and apparently of short stature, preceded people whose skeletal remains conform to the modern Salish ("Thompson River") sub-type. Occasional individuals of this ancient lower Fraser type appear as minor elements in historic Haida, Kwakiutl, and Coast Salish series. This probably means that this former population once occupied a considerable portion of the northern coasts.

An intriguing problem, which unfortunately probably cannot be resolved after more than a century and a half of racial mixture, relates to the occurrences of a few individuals with definitely brown (rather than the usual "very dark brown") hair color, and light-colored eyes. Alexander Mackenzie noted a number of such persons, with gray eyes, among the Bella Coola in 1793 (he was of course the first European known to have met this nation). We can only speculate as to whether these physical traits represent local mutations from the normal Northwest Coast genetic traditions, or whether some "Archaic White" strain, such as many human biologists believe occurs among the Ainu (the aborigines of Japan), might have been included in the racial heritage of the Northwest Coast Indians.

From western Washington south to northern California, there are few data on the Indian physical type or types. No studies were made in early days comparable to those by Boas in the north; since that time many small groups have dwindled to disappearance, and others have become so racially mixed that it would be impossible to define the aboriginal type. There are a few figures on stature, which show great irregularity, rather than a uniform trend as in the north. The Puget Sound Salish were in the medium category, with an average height of 165 centimeters—a little taller than their lower Fraser cousins. The Chinook on the Columbia were tall: 169 centimeters. The groups of the central Oregon coast seem to have been medium, around 165 centimeters; the northwest Californians varied from medium to tall. Some physical anthropologists have the impression that there was a strong strain of interior type, perhaps similar to Boas's "northern sub-type," in this region, which, in southwest Oregon and northwest California, was blended with a distinct longheaded California type.

HISTORY OF EUROPEAN CONTACTS

Aside from the apocryphal voyages of Juan de Fuca and Admiral Fuente, the first Europeans to see the Northwest Coast were the Russian crew of one of the vessels of the Dane Vitus Bering, who made landfall in Tlingit territory in 1741. They sent a boat ashore which never returned. Presumably the boat crew was killed by the Tlingit, because a number of war canoes came out to threaten the ship itself, whereupon Bering sailed away. In 1774 a Spaniard, Juan Perez, hove to at a place he called San Lorenzo, which seems to have been Nootka Sound. Some natives came out in canoes and were given a couple of silver spoons. These ephemeral contacts had little effect on the natives, of course. The first really important European contact occurred in 1778 on Captain James Cook's third voyage of exploration. He entered Nootka Sound where he spent some time before sailing on to southwest Alaska. While at Nootka Sound, some of Cook's party were given, and others traded for, sea-otter skins. When the expedition reached China, after Cook's tragic death in the Hawaiian Islands, they discovered that the lustrous brown pelts were highly prized by the Chinese, who were willing to pay—for that period—fabulous prices for them. When this news reached England, it was not long before a number of ships were fitting out for a voyage to the new land of treasure. Companies were formed in England for this new trade, and the East India Company assigned vessels to it. Hanna, Meares, Dixon, and Portlock were among the first ship captains to arrive on the coast. They explored hitherto unknown parts of it and then departed for China to dispose of their rich hauls of furs. For the next few years, dozens of vessels visited the coast annually. They combed the bays and inlets in search of Indians who might have sea-otter pelts. English and American ships, the latter principally out of Boston, dominated the trade. Before long two other nations who had Pacific interests became alarmed at what they considered a threat to their colonial empires.

The Russian-American Company had established its base on Kodiak Island in 1789. Up to that time, and for the next few years, the Russians confined their activities pretty much to the exploitation of the southwestern Alaskan fur trade; but the presence on the coast of so many vessels flying other flags eventually stimulated their expansion into Tlingit territory. Before this happened, however, in 1790, Spanish fear of the threat to her dominions created the so-called Nootka Controversy, which nearly brought England and Spain to war. These facts, of course, were of little immediate concern to the natives and are mentioned here only in passing. The effect of the fur trade on the native cultures is more important.

While Cook was in Nootka Sound, he noted that the Indians were quite familiar with iron, possessed a considerable number of tools and implements of this material, and—what proved of most importance to the later traders—were very anxious to acquire iron blades of any sort. For the next few years, the traders who succeeded Cook discovered that flat iron blades and chisels were the best possible trade goods. They filled their holds with pelts worth a king's ransom in China for a few barrels of adze blades, roughly made knives, and cheap glass beads given in exchange. However, they soon glutted the market, and in competing amongst themselves, taught the Indians to set higher and higher prices on their furs. Then there followed a period in which fads ruled the trade. A captain named Ingraham had his ship's armorer make some bracelets and neck rings of twisted wrought iron. These caught the native fancy and for a season or two following, the Indians spurned most other trade articles. The seafaring traders racked their brains to find things that might appeal to the Indians. Before long the Boston skippers came to dominate the trade. Their single great advantage was their ability to sell their cargoes directly in China. British traders could not take advantage of this because the East India Company held a monopoly on trade in Asiatic ports. The Yankee skippers developed an elaborate three-cornered operation. They sailed from Boston to the Northwest Coast, where they traded for furs which they sold in Canton and bought cargoes of tea, spices, and silk which they brought back to Boston. Eventually sandalwood from the Hawaiian Islands was included as a regular item for the Chinese trade.

The seagoing traders differed in one very important respect from traders ashore, who established posts which they planned to maintain for a number of years. The seafarers did not intend to return. The captain's share from a really successful voyage netted him enough to retire on, or at least enough to set him up in business ashore. Consequently, they had no interest in cultivating the good will of the natives. They did not hesitate to cheat or to rob them when they could obtain furs no other way. The warlike nature of the Northwest Coast Indians was their only deterrent from outright piracy. Even at that, there were innumerable affrays. Some traders fired at flotillas of canoes or villages on the beach at the slightest provocation; naturally, the Indians retaliated. If they could not revenge themselves on the attacking vessel, they were liable to assail the next ship that came along, for in their view all white men were of one tribe.

As time went on, faddism in trade goods decreased and utilitarian articles were in greater demand, as well as a few luxury items that included exotic foods like molasses, rice, and, of course, rum—the traders' standby. Firearms came into great demand. Some traders discovered that certain native products were reliable commodities, so they traded for tanned elkskins at the mouth of the Columbia and exchanged these for furs with the northern groups. Dentalia from Nootka territory, slaves from wherever they could be bought, and olachen oil from the Nass were all frequently carried aboard Boston vessels as trade goods.

Meanwhile, as the traders were stripping the coast of sea-otter furs, other events had taken place. Vancouver, in 1792 and 1793, had made his meticulous explorations and surveys and had discussed transfer of the Spanish establishment at Nootka to the British Crown with the Spanish commander Bodega y Quadra. The year 1793 marks the beginning of another era—that of the interest in the coastal trade that was ultimately demonstrated by land-based companies. The Northwest Company sent Alexander Mackenzie overland to search for a route of access to the coast. In 1799, the Russians established Fort Archangel near modern Sitka, which the Tlingit attacked and destroyed two years later. In 1804 the Russians made another attempt and built a new fort near the same site, which they were able to hold.

The pattern for the expansion of land-based fur traders on the Northwest Coast came into existence in 1821 with the coalition of the Hudson's Bay and the Northwest companies. Sir George Simpson was designated governor of the "Northern Department," which included

the Northwest Coast and the adjacent interior. The same year that
the headquarters of the Company was moved across the Columbia to
Fort Vancouver, at Simpson's orders a supply ship was sent to the Portland Canal, which had finally been established as the southern limit
of Russian claims in Northwest America. In the course of the next few
years, a chain of posts was built along the coast. Fort Langley, in the
vicinity of modern Vancouver, British Columbia, was built in 1827;
Fort Nass in 1831, abandoned and replaced by Fort Simpson in 1834,
and Fort McLoughlin in 1834. The purpose of the northern forts
was to cut off the flow of furs to the American traders. By this time,
the sea-otter population along the whole coast had been reduced to a
small fraction of its original abundance. The traders were dealing
mostly in land furs, beaver, land otter, and the like, that were obtained in the interior, traded to Indian middlemen on the coast, and
by them to the white fur buyers. The fact that the Indians knew a
good thing when they saw it was made abundantly clear to the representative of Hudson's Bay Company, Peter Skene Ogden, when he
went to survey the possibilities of establishing a post on the Stikine
River. Two Stikine Tlingit chiefs visited him and told him, in what
Ogden termed somewhat plaintively in his report "a tone I was not
in the habit of hearing," that they would not permit him to establish
a post upriver where it would be in a position to cut off their trade
with the interior. A more emphatic demonstration of their belief in
the importance of their monopolistic trade rights is reported to have
been made by the Chilkat Tlingit in 1852. This group sent a war
party nearly three hundred miles inland on a mission, successfully
carried out, of capturing and destroying the Hudson's Bay Company's
post of Fort Selkirk, at the junction of the Lewes and Pelly rivers.
The captured personnel of the post were not massacred, but humanely
released with the stern warning, however, that they should stay out
of Chilkat trading territory.

To return to the history of the coast, in 1839 the Hudson's Bay
Company leased the mainland coast of southeast Alaska, from Mount
Fairweather to the Portland Canal, from the Russians for a period of
ten years. They established posts at the mouth of the Stikine and the
Taku rivers. For the next few years, the policies of the Company,
which involved a minimum of direct interference with native cultures
—other than supplying the people with trade articles—prevailed for

the length of the coast. The Indians were enriched in worldly possessions and free to make such use of them as they pleased. More important still, the nations of southeast Alaska and coastal British Columbia remained, and remain to this day, on their ancestral sites and have never been subjected to the demoralizing effects of segregated reservation life.

TWO

ECONOMY

Fᴉsʜɪɴɢ ᴡᴀs the basis of Northwest Coast economy. The rivers and the sea provided an abundance of foods. There are five species of Pacific salmon, some of which "run" annually in every river and stream along the coast. All of these could be taken in great quantity to be dried and stored for future use. Smelt, herring, and, in the north, the oil-rich olachen or "candlefish" also assembled in vast numbers during their spawning seasons, and were easily caught by the Indians. A variety of efficient devices was used by Indian fishermen. Traps, constructed like huge baskets, were set up in the rivers and sometimes at points along the coast where salmon congregate. Fencelike weirs of poles were constructed to turn the fish into these traps (Figs. 2, 3). For olachen, wherever they run, a special type of funnel-shaped net was used from the Kwakiutl area northward. The principal "runs" are in the Nass, the Kitamat, and the Bella Coola rivers, and the main rivers emptying into Rivers and Knights inlets. Ownership of olachen-fishing rights was highly prized, and people from far and near assembled at places like the lower Nass River where Haida and Tlingit who had no fishing rights came to buy the oil.

All the coastal groups made dip nets, that is, bags of netting attached to a wooden frame on a handle, some like large editions of our fly fisherman's landing net, others on a V-shaped frame (Fig. 4). These were used for salmon, and, in finer mesh and specialized forms, for smaller fish like herring and smelt. Long sections of netting suitable for seining or gill-netting (a special form in which the mesh allows the fish's head to enter, but catches under his gill covers when he tries to turn back), or that could be fashioned into huge bags for trawling from canoes, appear to have been ancient devices among the Coast Salish and all the groups to the southward, but not along the northern coasts, with the possible exception of the Tsimshian Niska. The Coast Tsimshian and the Haida claim to have learned the use of the Niska gill nets—in fact, obtained the finished nets—from the people of the Nass in late prehistoric or early historic times.

The harpoon, a sort of spear with detachable head connected to the shaft by a short line, was one of the principal salmon-fishing devices. The northernmost groups used harpoons with a single, one-

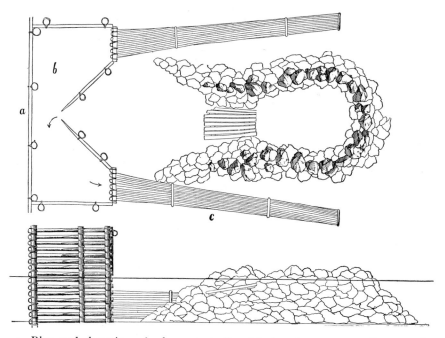

2. *Plan and elevation of salmon trap, Kwakiutl: a, fence, generally extends some distance beyond the low-water banks of the river; b, boxlike structure built of frames tied to stakes, in the middle of the river; c, on each side of the converging frames are two short frames with openings that lead into long, narrow fish baskets.*

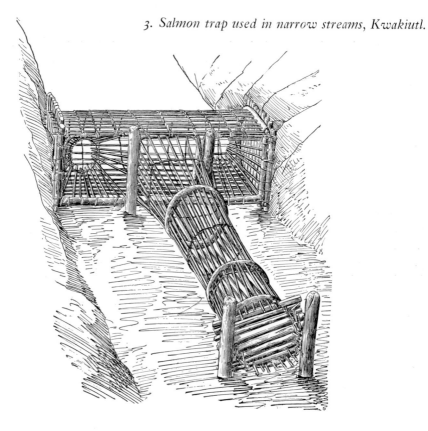

piece barbed bone or horn point; from Kwakiutl territory to north-western California two-pronged harpoons, armed with compound barbed heads, were used (Fig. 5). There were many variations on this two-pronged harpoon pattern, especially among the Kwakiutl-speaking groups and the Nootka. Lightweight short harpoons were made for throwing at salmon that swam with their dorsal fins out of the water in the bays near river mouths. Shafts that projected beyond the diverging foreshafts were used for thrusting downward in deep pools; the projecting main shaft served as a buffer, to protect the points from breaking on rocks in the river bottom. Leisters—poles with two springy arms fitted with sharp points projecting inward and backward—were common from the Gulf of Georgia northward. Nowadays detachable gaffs, made of a heavy-gauge steel hook attached to the shaft by a short lanyard, harpoon-fashion, are popular salmon-fishing implements.

Angling was another method of fishing. Salmon will strike a baited

26

hook while still in salt water, before the spawning season; cod and halibut will take bait at any time. The most nearly universally used hook was the simplest form, with a straight or slightly curved wooden shank to which a barbless bone or horn point was lashed at an acute angle (Fig. 6c). The groups living on the Olympic Peninsula above the Gulf of Georgia—the Nootka and Southern Kwakiutl—used such hooks, baited with fresh herring, in trolling for king salmon. Though a hand-line technique was used, it took no small measure of skill to boat a mature "king" (or "spring" or "Chinook" in colloquial terminology) on one of these barbless hooks. Cod were taken by bottom-fishing with the same type of hooks.

Halibut were taken by bottom-fishing, also, from the Olympic Peninsula north, but special hooks were used. The Tlingit, Haida, Tsimshian, and the Northern Kwakiutl groups, Haisla, and Xaihais, made halibut hooks of hardwood, shaped like a V with one short arm, with a bone barb fastened into the short side. The shanks of these hooks were often elaborately carved with crests or figures intended to have magical potency (Fig. 7). Two of these hooks were attached by short leaders to the ends of a cross-pole, to the middle of which a stone sinker was attached. The cross-pole held the buoyant wooden hooks clear of the line so as not to foul it. Large hooks of similar form,

4. Karok dip-netting salmon, lower Klamath River. Courtesy of A. L. Kroeber.

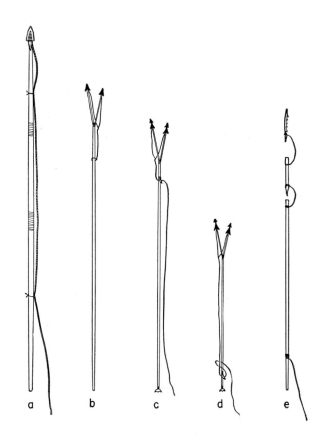

5. *Types of harpoons: a, Nootkan whaling harpoon assembly. The lanyard from the compound head was attached to the shaft at two points with light string, so that the weight of lanyard and long line to which it was attached would not pull the head from the shaft before it was thrust into the whale; b, common type of salmon harpoon, used everywhere except among the northern groups (who used a single tipped implement); the lanyards are joined and tied to the lower end of the shaft; c, older, and d, more recent types of sealing harpoons used by Kwakiutl and Nootka. The spurlike catches on the shafts held the heads in place during the harpoon's flight through the air; e, Northern-type sealing harpoon, with detachable foreshaft (parts are shown separated for clarity). Sometimes the line from the foreshaft was lengthened and attached to a float, rather than to the shaft. Note: Scale of the implements in this figure is approximately the same: the shortest, the recent Kwakiutl-Nootka type, being 6 to 7 feet long; the whaling harpoon from 14 to 18 feet long.*

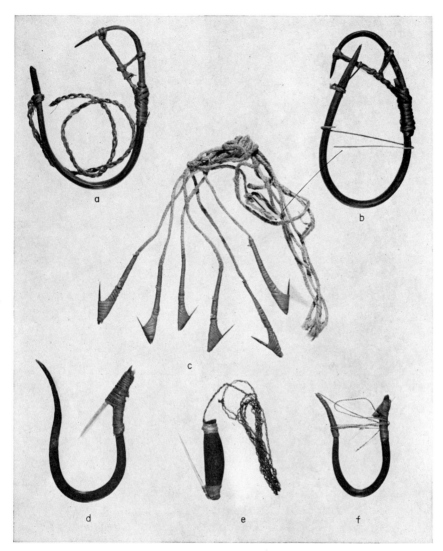

6. *Various types of fishhooks: a and b, Haida "black cod" hooks, also used by neighboring groups for ground fishing; c, sharp-angled hook of the type commonly used for codfish, and also for salmon-trolling. The specimens shown here are Tlingit; d and f, Kwakiutl-Nootka-type halibut hooks; the U-shaped shank was steamed and bent into shape; e, a Nootka type, used in offshore trolling for salmon. Some Nootka trolling hooks, made for baiting with whole herring, had slender shanks like those of c. The wrappings across the two arms of hooks b and f were put on when the hooks were not in use, to keep them in shape.*

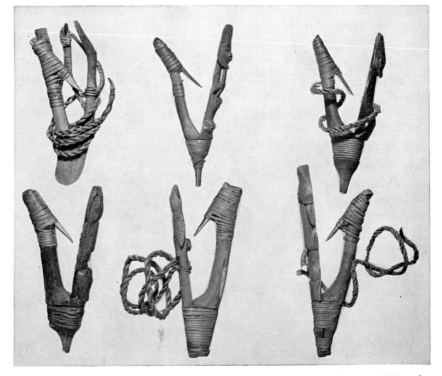

7. *Tlingit and Haida V-shaped halibut hooks. Coast Tsimshian and Northern Kwakiutl made and used the same type.*

but undecorated, were used by the Chinook for the huge Columbia River sturgeon. The other Kwakiutl-speaking tribes, the Nootka, the Coast Salish of the Gulf of Georgia and Puget Sound, and the groups of northwestern Washington, made halibut hooks of spruce withes, steamed into U shape, and fitted with a sharp bone barb (Fig. *6d, f*). The springy arms of the hook spread to permit the halibut to insert his snout to take the bait, then helped set the barb. These hooks were attached to one end of a short rod, the other end of which was made fast to the line, and also supported a stone weight just heavy enough to hold the rod horizontally, and keep the hook clear of the line. Lines were commonly made of the long thin stems of giant kelp.

A number of other minor fishing devices were also in use along the coast. The "herring rake," for example, was a long flat board with sharp bone points set in one edge. While a companion in the stern paddled, the fisherman used the rake with a paddling motion, holding it edgewise, points to the rear. As the canoe glided over the surfacing shoals of herring, the fisherman followed through on each stroke so as to bring the rake over the gunwale behind him, shaking the fish impaled on the points into the canoe. This device was used for olachen fishing by the Niska before they learned to make and use the special funnel-shaped nets from the Haida, according to local traditions.

In the Puget Sound area and along the Washington coast one's feet and a sharp stick were all one needed to catch flounders. Parties of men and youths waded about on the mud flats. When the fisherman stepped on a flatfish resting on the bottom, he tried to hold the fish until he could spear it with the stick. This sort of fishing was considered something of a lark.

The northwestern Californians made a simple gaff by lashing a

8. *Haida hardwood clubs for dispatching hooked halibut and harpooned seal. Tlingit, Tsimshian, and Northern Kwakiutl used similar implements; farther south, shaped but undecorated clubs were used.*

sharp splinter of bone to a long pole, and with this tool hooked out the lamprey eels that run at certain seasons in the rivers.

In addition to the many varieties of fish, the sea also provided numerous edible shellfish: clams of many kinds, mussels, small abalones, and, in some localities, oysters, and a great host of small gastropods such as limpets and periwinkles. Crabs, sea urchins, and the like were also abundant. That the Indians did not disdain these delicacies is proved by the fact that old village sites from Yakutat to Trinidad Bay are marked by great mounds consisting mostly of the shells discarded after meals made of the shellfish. Some shells also provided useful materials for tools or utensils. Large mussel shells were ground sharp to form the areally universal woman's knife. Deep clamshells made convenient spoons for sipping broth. Gathering shellfish was generally regarded as a woman's task, although men occasionally aided their wives. Specially made sticks of hardwood were used to dig up the mollusks or pry them loose.

While the hunting of sea mammals had a definite economic value, it yielded even greater returns in prestige to its participants. Among many of the tribes it approached a professional status; specific types of sea hunting were specialties of high-ranking chiefs. Chiefs of Northern Nootkan and most Kwakiutl tribes had special hereditary rights to the fat and flesh of hair seal taken in their waters, indicating the great importance they attached to sealing.

Hair seal, sea lion, and porpoise were hunted with the same type of equipment by most of the tribes. Special canoes, slim-waisted, with racy lines, were usually built for sea hunting. The hulls were scorched to remove splinters and sanded down to a glassy smoothness with sharkskin to permit them to slip through the water swiftly and noiselessly. Among the three northernmost groups, the harpoon had a single foreshaft with a long multiple-barbed bone point. Some were made with a detachable foreshaft: the point was connected to the foreshaft by a short lanyard, the foreshaft to the shaft by another, and the shaft carried a long line which the harpooner held or made fast to a canoe thwart (Figs. 5e, 9d). These several joints produced a sort of shock-absorber effect when the struck quarry lunged, minimizing the strain on each individual part. The northwestern Californians used a similar harpoon point, set in a socket in a very heavy shaft, to kill sea lions. The line was wrapped about the shaft for its full length and made fast to it so the shaft acted as a drogue, tiring the animal while the hunters

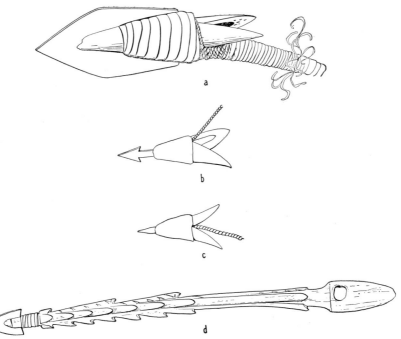

9. Various types of harpoon heads (detail): a, Nootkan whaling harpoon head; b, Kwakiutl-Nootka sealing harpoon (of historic type, with iron cutting blade); c, typical three-piece salmon harpoon head; d, Northern-type sealing harpoon head (most Tlingit, Haida, and Tsimshian salmon harpoons were of the same general type but much less ornate).

followed. The groups living between the two extremes of the area used harpoons with two diverging foreshafts, on each of which was mounted a three-piece head with a sharp blade bound between two horn barbs. The line was held in place by a catch on the shaft, and extended from there to a coil that the harpooner paid out as he threw, just as a cowhand pays out a lasso in roping. Kwakiutl and Nootka sea hunters, and some neighboring Salish who had learned from them, did not throw these harpoons javelin-fashion, but steadied the shaft with the left hand (which also held the coil of line), and applied the propulsive thrust to the end of the shaft. Some Kwakiutl hunters fitted a butt-piece on to their harpoon shafts, with two perforations through which the hunter put his index and middle fingers; others, like the Nootka, achieved the same end by fitting a little tridentlike finger rest of bone (Fig. 5c, d). These devices, and the whole throwing technique, probably gave better control, and also suggest the possibility that they may be modifications of the Eskimo atlatl, or throwing board. The harpooner struck his prey, played it as a modern fly fisherman plays a husky rainbow trout; finally, he pulled it alongside his canoe, dispatched it with a club, and then boated it. Sometimes a sealskin float would be made fast to the end of the line in sea-lion hunting, and allowed to run until the quarry tired. Small floats made of seal or sea-lion bladders were fastened to the line by Southern Kwakiutl for all sea hunting, while some Heiltsuk used sealskin floats similar to those of the Nootka. In hunting porpoise, floats were always used by these groups, for the skin of the animal was so thin that too heavy a strain would probably cause the harpoon head to draw. Their neighbors did not use these buoys.

Sea otter, whose dense, lustrous pelts were so avidly sought after by European traders, were formerly hunted like hair seal. With the intensification of the trade, and the dwindling of the sea otter, mass hunts came into vogue, in which twenty or thirty or more canoes made sweeps along the coast, forming up in a circle around any sea otter sighted. Each time the animal surfaced volleys of arrows were loosed at it until it was killed. The efficiency of this broad coverage-and-surround technique is attested by the fact that the sea otter almost became extinct by the end of the last century.

Fur seal were probably unknown to most Northwest Coast Indians in aboriginal times, for the migration route of the herds is farther offshore than the natives ventured. The Haida and Coast Tsimshian were the main exceptions: they pursued the numerous stragglers from the main herd who came into Dixon Entrance to follow Hecate Strait between the Queen Charlotte Islands and the mainland. American and Canadian sealers began to recruit hunters, particularly among the Nootka and Kwakiutl, in the closing decades of the nineteenth century. From that time until the signing of the international conservation treaty regulating fur-seal hunting, shipping on sealing schooners came close to becoming a national industry for those two peoples.

The most spectacular sea hunting on the whole coast was the whaling of the Nootka and their neighbors of the Olympic Peninsula —Quileute, Quinault, Klallam, and perhaps the Chemakum, all of whom learned the art from the Nootkans. The whale harpooner was always a person of high rank, for the tricks of the trade—practical and

magical—that contributed to the success of the hunt were cherished
family secrets, handed down in noble lines only. Besides, only a chief
possessed the necessary wealth to have a whaling canoe built, to outfit it,
and the authority to assemble a crew. The whaling harpoon was a very
specialized piece of equipment (Figs. 5a, 9a). The harpoon head was
made of three pieces: a sharp mussel-shell cutting blade cemented with
spruce gum between two heavy elkhorn barbs. A heavy lanyard of
sinew twisted into rope connected the head of the 100-fathom-long
line laid up of cedar withes. Four sealskin buoys were attached to the
line at intervals. In historic times a huge reinforced cedarbark basket,
in which the line was coiled, was made fast to the bitter end and served
as a drogue, but this apparently was an improvisation modeled after
the drogues of white seafarers.

The crew, with all the gear stowed according to a meticulous
pattern so that the line and floats would run out without fouling,
paddled out to sea. When they sighted a whale, they tried to approach
silently from the rear so the animal would neither hear nor see them.
They always came in on the whale's left side. The canoe had to lay
close alongside, for the harpoon was much too heavy to be thrown,
and had to be thrust home. The harpooner stood with his left foot
on the bow thwart, his right forward on the gunwale, with the harpoon held crosswise in front of him at about shoulder height. He
pivoted and struck, aiming just behind the cetacean's left flipper, then
ducked down into the forward compartment as the whale rolled and
thrashed about and the canoe sheered off hard to port, to avoid being
struck by the floats or springy coil of line as they paid out. This was
the most dangerous moment. The whale might turn toward the canoe,
smashing it to bits in one of his blind rushes; a crewman might be
badly injured by a blow from a float or the rigid line, or even be
caught in a bight and dragged to his death. It was mainly for this
moment that the whaler and his crew practiced long drill sessions and
carried out arduous rituals of ceremonial purification to forestall any
mishaps. On the beach, their families also observed certain rituals
for their good luck and welfare. Ritual behavior before and during the
hunt was considered essential for all sea hunting, of course, but because
of the importance of whaling in native eyes its ceremonial require-
ments were more elaborate and more rigid than those for any other
quest.

Usually a second whaling canoe, captained by a kinsman of the chief whaler, accompanied the hunt and often was conceded the privilege of planting the second harpoon. A small, swift sealing canoe might also be brought along, to take the first harpoon shaft back to the village as formal evidence that a whale had been struck. The whaler and his supporting canoe then followed the whale, running in to drive home more harpoons with short lines and floats, until the great creature was so weakened by loss of blood, the drag of the floats, and its titanic struggles that it lay quiet in the water as the hunter came in for the kill. A lance with a very wide chisel-like blade, much like a white whaler's "spade," was used to sever the tendons controlling the flukes, so that the cetacean lay hamstrung and helpless. Then another lance with a long sharp bone point was driven home behind the flipper to the heart. The cetacean rolled, spouted blood, and died. Holes were hacked through the upper lip and around the lower jaw to tie the mouth shut, so the carcass would not ship water and sink. Then all that remained was the wearisome chore of towing the quarry home. If luck was with the hunter, or, as the Indians interpreted it, if he and his crew had been punctilious in carrying out their rituals, the whale, when struck, would turn toward shore so it could be killed close to the beach. But frequently whales headed straight out to sea, so the crew had to pay for their ritual laxness by a day or more of steady paddling.

It is interesting to note that much of the impedimenta of the Nootka whale hunt, including the use of a special large canoe, harpoons with long lines and sealskin floats, the prestige associated with whaling, and many ritual elements to be described below, are very reminiscent of Eskimo whaling practices. Another kind of Nootkan whaler, or better, whale-ritualist, did not even approach the creatures at sea, but magically caused whales that had died from natural causes to drift ashore. Formerly Aleut whalers, in *bidarkas*, hurled lances with poisoned slate blades into whales, then went ashore to perform ceremonies to cause the carcasses to drift in. While the Aleut actually killed his whale and the Nootka whale-ritualist did not, the rites each performed in secret in some secluded spot were much alike. Both sets of ceremonies involved the use of human skeletons or corpses, who were supposed to call to the whale, or were propped up holding a line attached to an effigy of a whale. The basic idea was that through his rituals, songs, and prayers, each whale-ritualist induced the spirits of the dead to bring the whale ashore. The fact that the Nootka practiced both techniques of northern whaling (although such groups as the Tlingit, Haida, and Tsimshian knew nothing of them, even though they were geographically closer to Eskimo and Aleut) suggests some ancient connection between the Nootka and subarctic and arctic cultures.

Other Northwest Coast groups, although they did not use the same magical methods for causing whales that died from natural causes to drift ashore, enthusiastically utilized such bonanzas of oil-rich blubber and meat, "high" though the carcasses might be. Only the Tlingit turned up their noses, literally and figuratively, at dead whales washed up on their beaches.

Land hunting was practiced to a limited extent only, by most Northwest Coast tribes. It was of major importance to communities and small tribes living at some distance up the river valleys, away from salt water. The Chilkat Tlingit, for example, hunted a good deal and staged many caribou hunts on their trading trips into the interior. The Tsimshian division of the upper Nass River, who in former days are said to have come below the head of tidewater only rarely, are claimed to have been great hunters, as were the related Gitksan on the upper Skeena. Men of the upper Bella Coola villages, the Wikeno of Wikeno Lake above Rivers Inlet, and a few Nootka who lived on Gold River and about Sproat Lake were good woodsmen and hunters of land game. Up the Fraser and on the upper reaches of the rivers draining into Puget Sound lived Coast Salish whose way of life and economy was almost more like that of the Interior Salish than like those of their congeners and blood kinsmen downriver and along the coast. Lewis and Clark report that the Upper Chinook hunted antelope on the plains of eastern Oregon and Washington. The upriver Yurok, the Karok, and Hupa as well, hunted extensively.

Naturally, hunting techniques and equipment varied both according to the game sought and the terrain. In the south, from the central Washington coast down to northwest California, while snares and deadfalls were known, pitfall traps were commonly set for elk, deer, and black bear. Farther north, where the soils are shallow and rocky, pitfalls were rare, and snares and deadfalls (Fig. 10) were used almost exclusively. The bow and arrow was, of course, the standard land-hunting arm everywhere before the introduction of firearms, but pikes were also used on certain large game. Even the ordinary canoe paddle became a hunting weapon among the salt-water groups. If a canoeman

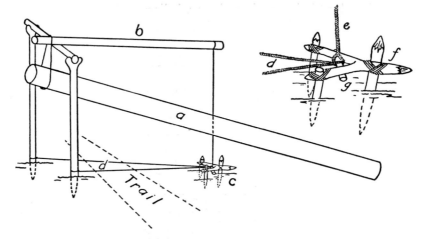

10. Diagram of type of deadfall trap used by Nootka for deer: a, heavy log which drops on the quarry; b, crossbar supporting one end of the log and connected to the trigger (c) by the other end; d, the kick lines that trip the trigger and release the weight; the inset shows the detail of the trigger; d, again represents the trip lines that pull the small crosspiece (g) out through the open arms of the forked branch (f) thus releasing line (e) and the crossbar to which it is connected. Courtesy of Smithsonian Institution.

encountered any land animal—deer, elk, bear, or the like—swimming across the channel, he overtook it, clubbed it with his paddle until he could hold its head under water with the same instrument to drown it, then rolled his quarry aboard, and continued on his way.

For waterfowl there were a variety of special devices: underwater traps with baited gorges for diving ducks, used by most Kwakiutl and Nootka divisions; small throwing nets mounted on pole frames that could be used from canoes on black stormy nights; spears tipped with many long diverging hardwood points that increased coverage like the spread of shot of a shotgun, favored by the Gulf of Georgia, Olympic Peninsula, and perhaps some Puget Sound groups. Many Coast Salish also made long nets (or perhaps used their long salmon seines and gill nets), stretching them across flyways between lakes and ponds where ducks were accustomed to come in low. The northwest Californian deerstalker used a device common to many of his non-coastal neighbors to the south and east—he wore a stuffed deer-head disguise on his head, so that, imitating the movements of a browsing

deer, he could move in close enough for a perfect shot without alarming his victim.

Certain land animals, within the limits of their range, were
especially prized for their hides or other parts, and their successful
hunting gave considerable prestige. Among the mainland groups, from
the Chilkat south to the Gulf of Georgia, the mountain goat was highly
esteemed for its "wool," for even though the Chilkat was the only
group of late historic times to weave all-wool blankets, their neighbors all prized yellow-cedar robes with a few strands of woolen yarn
run in. The jet-black horns were used to make spoons. The mountain
goat is a wary animal, difficult even for the modern hunter with a
high-powered rifle and telescopic sights. The Indian goat hunter,
with his companions and their trained dogs, sought to climb above the
animals and, without unnecessarily alarming them, gradually work
them down from the cliffs into the rock slides, and if possible, into
some cul-de-sac, or through some narrow sheer-walled pass in which
snares could be set, or where companions could lie in wait. Such
places were very valuable properties and were held by individual
chiefs for their lineages. The usual weapon carried was a short hardwood pike, sometimes merely sharpened to a point, sometimes mount-
ing a horn or bone blade. Apparently if a hunter ever maneuvered
the goats to a place where he could get within bowshot, he could
as easily close to spear-thrusting distance; besides, in inching along the
goat trails on the cliffs and scrambling over rock slides, the more
fragile bow and arrows were more liable to be damaged than the
sturdy pike.

Skins of the whistling marmot were regarded as very valuable,
particularly among Tlingit, Haida, Tsimshian, and the northern Kwakiutl divisions. It seems that anciently a robe made by sewing together many of the small soft-furred hides was about equal in value
to a sea-otter robe. Hunters from the mainland groups climbed high
above timberline to set deadfall traps around the marmot dens. Bone
"triggers," carved with figures believed to have magical power, were
made especially for these traps.

In northwestern California, the prize of prizes was an albino
deer. The hide of such an animal, decorated with scarlet scalps of the
pileated woodpecker and mounted so that it could be carried on a pole
in the wealth-display ceremonies, was a treasure of tremendous worth.
The lucky hunter who brought down one of these deer thereby took

a major initial step on the road to greatness for himself and his family.

Over the larger part of the area, vegetable foods were comparatively few and unimportant in the native diet. North of Puget Sound there are few plants that produce and store large amounts of starch in seeds or tubers. The rather spindly roots of a kind of clover, and the tough fibrous ones of bracken fern, were dug occasionally to lend some variety to the diet. The "inner bark"—apparently the cambium layer—of various trees was scraped and eaten by most groups, from the Kwakiutl northward. All in all, however, few sources of starchy foods were available. It has even been suggested that the great emphasis on oils and fats in the northern Northwest Coast dietary may have developed to compensate for the dearth of starches. Certainly these Indians had no innate dislike for starchy foods: they promptly acquired a taste for white men's bread, flour, and potatoes, and since early historic times have planted potato patches on ancient middens whose alkaline soil seems well adapted to this crop.

Berries of various kinds are fairly abundant, and they were utilized by all the tribes. The berries were eaten fresh, either plain or mixed with olachen or whale oil, or preserved. For storing, the berries were cooked to a pulpy mass, poured into rectangular wooden frames lined with skunk-cabbage leaves, and dried into cakes. Another storing technique was to stir them into a mixture of year-old olachen grease and cold water.

In the southern part of our area two plants that stored starchy materials in quantities were abundant enough to become staple foods. One of these was camas (*Camassia quamash*). On the upper reaches of rivers flowing into Puget Sound, and from western Washington down the Oregon coast, "camas prairies" occur, and the Indians dug quantities of the roots for food. Farther down the coast, in southwest Oregon and northwest California, native housewives collected acorns in the oak groves, soaked and hulled them, ground them to a meal in shallow stone mortars with basketry hoppers, leached the bitter tannins out of the meal, and cooked it into a nourishing, if rather tasteless, gruel.

In addition to being boiled in watertight boxes or baskets, food was steam-cooked in large shallow pits filled with hot stones by placing it on the stones and covering the whole affair with leaves and mats, then pouring water through to the stones. Fish and meat were also broiled over an open fire, or over a bed of coals. That the cooking techniques were few and simple does not mean that the native diet was monotonous. A Kwakiutl housewife recorded some 150 different recipes for an anthropologist around the turn of the century, and there is no indication that her repertoire was exhausted. The long feast mats were unrolled to serve as tablecloths. From the Olympic Peninsula northward, dishes were larger and more elaborately carved; sometimes four, six, or eight men would be seated at a single dish. Ladles for serving food and oil were also decorated with crests of the host's family, and spoons of mountain-goat horn, carved and spread open by steaming, were distributed among the guests. The three northernmost tribes made huge decorated ladles of mountain-sheep horn, traded from the interior. For napkins, bundles of softly shredded cedarbark were prepared and distributed.

THREE

MATERIAL CULTURE

TECHNOLOGY AND MATERIALS

From the northernmost to the southern extreme of the area, the Indians utilized wood as a primary material for most of their manufactures. The products of their carpentry were distinguished by neatness of finish and, among the northern groups, by elaborate carved and painted decoration. This typical excellent workmanship was accomplished with what would strike most of us as a rather limited tool kit (Figs. 11–16). Chisels of tough stone such as nephrite, or of elkhorn, or of the dense shell of deep-water clams, mounted in hardwood hafts, were driven with unhafted pear-shaped stone mauls for felling timbers. The three northern nations—the Tlingit, Haida, and Tsimshian—sometimes used heavy chopping adzes in their aboriginal logging. Big logs were split, or sections were split from standing trees, by driving up sets of wedges—usually of hardwood, such as yew, with grommets of tough spruce root wrapped around the butt ends to prevent splitting. The northwestern Californians and their immediate neighbors made wedges of elkhorn. The unhafted maul (Fig. 13) was usually used for driving wedges, except in the north, where heavy hafted stone mauls were used by the three northernmost divisions, and by some of their Heiltsuk and Bella Coola neighbors. Besides the heavy splitting adzes just mentioned, three types of small

42

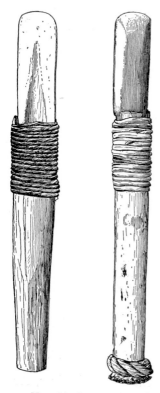

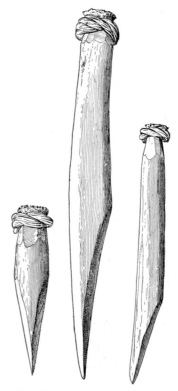

11. Kwakiutl woodworking tools: chisels.

12. Kwakiutl woodworking tools: wedges of yew wood.

13. Kwakiutl woodworking tools: stone hand hammers.

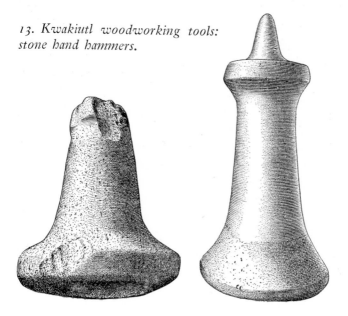

43

adzes served for the fine work. Although their distributions over-
lapped slightly, the "elbow adze" in which the cutting blade was lashed
to a T-shaped wooden handle was essentially northern, used by all
the groups from Tlingit through the Southern Kwakiutl; the "D-
adze" (Fig. 14), in which the handle, of wood or whalebone, was
shaped something like one of our handsaw handles, was common in
the central region, used by the Southern Kwakiutl and the Nootka
and their neighbors down the coast of Washington. South of the
Columbia a "straight adze," which looked more like a chisel with a
slightly curved handle, was in use. The Indians did a great part of
their carving with these adzes, planing rough wood to smooth, flat,
or curved surfaces, or to a decorated fluted finish. For the very finest
carving short curved blades mounted in wooden handles, something
like the Eskimo "crooked knife," were used. Anciently, the blades
may have been of ground-down beaver incisors, but for many years,
even before the coming of Europeans, iron was used. At Nootka
Captain Cook noted that most of the knives and chisels were iron-
tipped, and iron was eagerly sought after by the natives whom the
early fur traders encountered from Tlingit territory to Trinidad Bay
in California. Some ethnologists and historians have suggested that this
pre-European iron may have been found in the form of spikes, etc.,
from the wreckage of ships washed up on the beaches by the Japanese
Current, and there is evidence that such "drift iron" was used in
early historic times. However, few vessels in which iron spikes and
bolts were commonly used were sailing the western Pacific before
Cook's day. It is more likely that the same Siberian Iron Age center
that provided the Punuk culture of the archaeologically ancient Alaskan
Eskimo with metal was the ultimate source of prehistoric iron tools
on the Northwest Coast. Simple drills, with a short cutting bit fastened
into the end of a wooden handle that the carpenter rotated between
his palms, were used for drilling holes.

Fire was an important woodworking tool, strange as it may sound.
The Indians had effective techniques for controlling burning, and were
able to hollow out large logs with fire, in the manufacture of canoes
and the large troughlike feast dishes. Only the Kwakiutl and Nootka
claim to have scorned use of this method, for they hollowed out their
canoes, etc., with adzes and chisels. The softening effect of hot water
on wood was well known; it was a common practice to widen the
beam of a new canoe by filling it with water, throwing in red-hot

14. (Left) Kwakiutl woodworking tool: adze with bone blade.

15. (Below) Kwakiutl woodworking tools: crooked knives with metal blades. The upper sheath is made of wood, the lower of fawnskin.

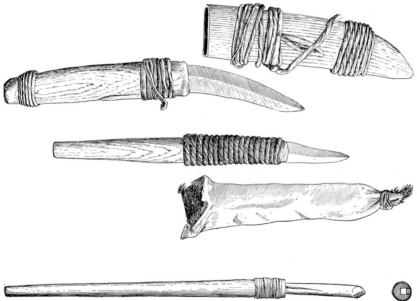

16. Kwakiutl wood-carving tool: drill and its cross-section. The handle is cedarwood, the point is bone.

stones until the water was almost boiling, then carefully driving in thwartlike spreaders from gunwale to gunwale. The Kwakiutl even had a device for softening small pieces of wood to bend and shape them that came close to the steam box of the modern boatwright. They also made molds in which steam-softened pieces of wood—for example, the shanks of the curved halibut hooks—were forced and left to set into the desired shape. To achieve the typical smooth neat finish on wooden articles, fine sandstone, and then sharkskin, were used in lieu of sandpaper.

In a sense, the natural environment favored development of the woodworking craft, for the towering forests of the Northwest contained a number of useful and readily workable woods. The red cedar (*Thuja plicata*), which splits easily into wide straight planks, served a multitude of purposes (in northwest California the equally tractable coast redwood [*Sequoia sempervirens*] was used for the same purposes); yellow cedar (*Chamaecyparis nootkaensis*) and alder (*Alnus* sp.) were the sources of material when soft, easily carved wood without marked cleavage planes was needed, as in the manufacture of dishes and masks. Where tough, resilient wood was desired—for example, for bows, harpoon foreshafts, and the like—few better woods could be found than yew (*Taxus brevifolia*) or, in the southern part of the area, maple (*Acer* sp.) and oak (*Quercus* sp.). Only the more northerly Tlingit groups—those residing north of modern Wrangel on the mainland shore, and from Admiralty Island northward offshore, beyond the limits of distribution of red and yellow cedar—had to make shift with less easily split hemlock for planks, and tough but untractable spruce for canoe hulls, when they could not trade for good cedar from their southern kinsmen.

Another important material, particularly from the Columbia River northward, was the inner bark of the red cedar and, to a slightly lesser degree, that of yellow cedar. Even the northerly Tlingit, in whose territory neither red nor yellow cedar grew, found it necessary to import quantities of the bark, as well as of the lumber, of the two trees. One could very nearly describe the life of the individual Indian in terms of cedarbark: as an infant, he was swaddled in the bark, shredded and haggled to a cottony consistency; his pillow and head-presser were pads of the same material; woven robes and rain capes of shredded bark protected him from rain and cold throughout his life; checkerwork mats of red cedarbark were his principal household furnishings, serving as tablecloths at mealtimes, as upholstery for seats, and as mattresses for his bed. With the beginning of European contacts he learned to use sails on his canoe; when he was unable to acquire imported canvas, he made sails of heavily woven bark mats; old worn-out mats served to protect his canoe from the checking effects of the sun on bright days. On ceremonial and festive occasions he wore turbans and arm and leg bands twisted and woven of shredded bark. He stowed his carpentering tools in a basket woven of the same bark. The Nootka whale hunter kept his precious harpoon heads in neatly made pouches of the same material. In historic times, our typical Northwest Coast native found shredded cedarbark to be an ideal gun wadding for the muzzle-loader he acquired from the white trader. And when he died, the chances were that unless he were a chief and entitled to special treatment, his body would be wrapped in a cedarbark mat for burial.

Most of this bark was stripped off standing trees. It is interesting to note that there was a conscious effort at conservation: only rarely was a tree stripped completely; instead, only part of the bark was removed, to permit the tree to recover and continue its growth. Long strips were pulled off, starting from a horizontal cut made near the base of the tree. Then the outer bark was peeled off and the inner bark rolled up into bales for carrying home. When dried, the red cedar-bark was split into strips for mat- and basketmaking, or shredded by feeding it across the edge of an old paddle blade and haggling it with a heavy blunt chopper of hardwood or whalebone (Figs. 17, 18). The

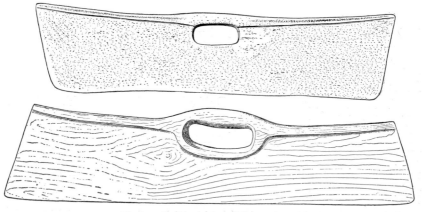

17. Red cedarbark shredders, Kwakiutl.

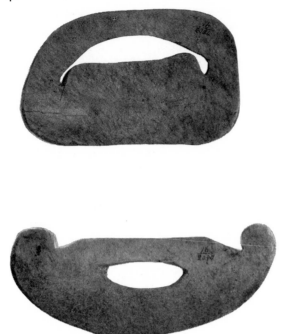

18. (Above) Cedarbark shredders of whalebone, Nootka.

19. (Right) Coast Salish mat needles.

bark of yellow cedar was treated by soaking it alternately in salt and fresh water, drying it, then pounding it with a whalebone or stone hammer until the fibers separated.

The Salish groups from the Gulf of Georgia southward, and their Chinook neighbors along the lower Columbia, substituted sewn mats of tules, or reeds, for the cedarbark mats of the northern neighbors. They passed a strand of twine through a flat row of reeds with a long wooden needle resembling an oversize sack needle, then crimped the reeds down with a special tool (Figs. 19, 20) to prevent the stems from cracking where the needle had split them. The use of this technique spread during historic times to adjacent Kwakiutl and Nootka who had access to stands of reeds around lakes and muskeg swamps; such mats are softer and more resilient than those of cedarbark.

The regional flora provided a variety of materials for basket weaving. The same red cedarbark used for mats served for flexible but strong baskets, woven with flat strips; for more rigid, tighter construction the same material was spun into stiff cord. Spruce roots, from which long wiry segments could be split, were widely used also. The bark of a "wild cherry" (*Prunus* sp.), various tough grasses, and a glossy black fern stem were frequently utilized for decorative patterns.

For textiles, in addition to the yellow cedarbark already noted, a few animal fibers were used. From Vancouver Island northward, mountain-goat wool was in great demand for weaving. The Salish groups of the Gulf of Georgia and on the shores of the Straits of Juan de Fuca had a special breed of little dogs whose wool-like hair they clipped to make into yarns for robes. However, the amounts of these animal fibers used were very small in comparison with those of vegetable origin.

20. Coast Salish mat creasers.

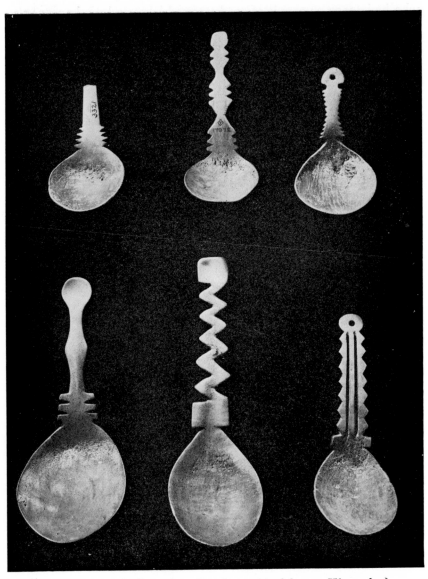

21. Yurok spoons of elk antler, showing typical lower Klamath decora-tion.

Other materials were used for special purposes, of course. Cutting blades made of stone and shell have been mentioned. A tough, hard, bright-green nephrite found in southeast Alaska and along the Fraser River was extensively used for adze blades. Horn and bone were ground down for many purposes. The use of the heavy shafts of elkhorn for wedges in northwest California has been noted. In the same region, neat little purses for shell money were carved of sections of elkhorn, as well as spoons for acorn mush, decorated with geometric designs (Fig. 21). Both horn and bone, particularly the compact hard material from the cannon bones of elk and deer, were used to make harpoon- and arrowpoints, and perhaps in pre-iron times, served for the blades of adzes and other tools. Along the northern mainland shore, horn of both mountain sheep and mountain goat was used for various purposes, after being softened in boiling water to permit shaping and molding. Some of the horn spoons and ladles of the Tlingit, Haida, Tsimshian, and Heiltsuk (Figs. 22–24), with their elaborately carved decoration, are veritable works of art. The Chinook, who acquired mountain-sheep horn from some distant source tapped by their trade connections, made very distinctively shaped dishes of the same material (Fig. 25).

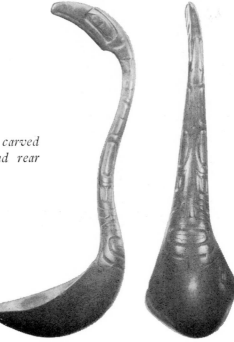

22. Tlingit ladle of shaped and carved mountain-sheep horn, side and rear views.

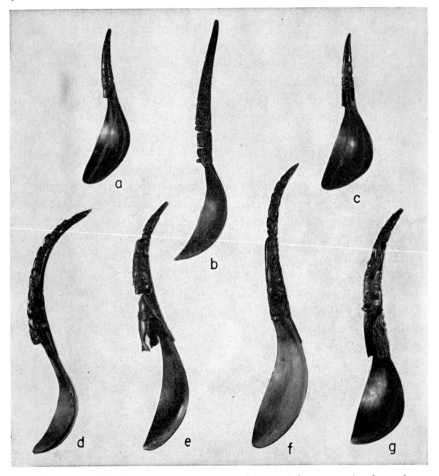

23. *Spoons and ladles of mountain-goat horn with mountain-sheep horn bowls (b, e, f), and all of mountain-goat horn (a, b, c, g); a and c are Tsimshian; remainder are Haida.*

Stoneworking was definitely a minor art on the Northwest Coast. Chipped stone was uncommon, except in the southern part of the area. There, along the Klamath River, huge, flaked blades of obsidian, as evenly and finely worked as any in the world, were made—not for utility but as valuables, comparable to crown jewels. Delicately flaked arrowpoints of chalcedony and agate, tiny and jewel-like in their

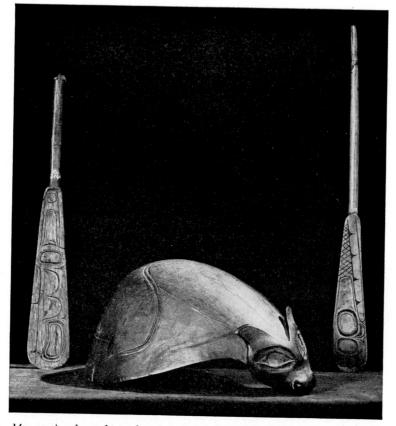

24. *Mountain-sheep horn bowl and wooden "sopalalli-berry" spoons. The flat spatulalike spoons were used to eat the popular sopalalli or "soapberry" mixture, consisting of the berries whipped up to a meringuelike stiff froth in a mixture of cold water and olachen grease. The carving on the dish is probably Tlingit, representing a Wolf, or Sea-wolf; the crosshatching on the right-hand spoon suggests reference to a Beaver; that on the left-hand spoon cannot be interpreted.*

perfection, were used by the Chinookan groups of the lower Columbia, but were trade articles made by the upriver interior tribes. Farther north, ground slate blades are found in archaeological sites, where, at the dawn of history, ground shell knives and harpoon blades

25. Chinook-style bowls of moun-tain-sheep horn. These particular specimens were collected from the Salish-speaking Quinault on the Washington Coast, but were un-doubtedly obtained in trade from the Columbia River. Courtesy of Smithsonian Institution.

were more common. In addition to the stone adze blades, mauls both hafted and unhafted, previously mentioned, and the large, flat pile drivers with prepared grips used by the Kwakiutl and Bella Coola for driving stakes for fish weirs, a few stone vessels—paint-grinding mortars, "oil dishes," and in the extreme south, shallow mortars used with basket hoppers for grinding acorns—were made. The lower Klamath River groups also made pipe bowls, set in tubular wooden stems, or, rarely, tubular stone pipes, for smoking their tobacco.

MANUFACTURES

Of the materials just discussed, wood served for houses, canoes, storage vessels, dishes, cooking utensils, cradles, and even—in the south—for pillows. The areally typical wooden houses fall into a series of regional subpatterns. In the north, the Tlingit, Haida, Tsimshian, and the Northern Kwakiutl-speaking Haisla built large rectangular gable-

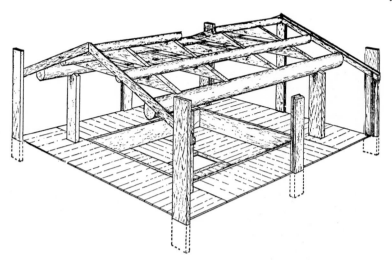

26. *Diagram of Northern house type, showing joined construction. Courtesy of University Museum, University of Pennsylvania.*

roofed houses, the elements of which were joined together. Heavy horizontal members, or plates, ran from corner post to corner post. These timbers had deep channels or slots cut into them—the ground plates along the upper side, and the roof plates on their lower sides—into which the ends of the vertically placed wall planks of cedar fitted (Figs. 26–28). Huge ridgepoles were supported by heavy posts at front and back; these in turn supported the overlapping layers of roof planking. The doorway, in the gable end facing the beach, was often in the form of a round or oval hole cut through the center post. Particularly among the Haida, an elaborately carved exterior post that extended high above the roof was set up in front of the house, and the gaping mouth of some crest figure formed the entrance. In many of these houses a deep pit was dug some feet inside of the walls; in fact, traditions tell of houses of renowned chiefs that had a series of four or five benches or steps. Across the back of the house, on the bench at ground level, if it had a deep central pit, and sometimes along the sides, were the sleeping compartments of the important families occupying it. These were small cubicles built of planks—miniatures, even to their gabled roofs, of the house. The front of the house-chief's compartment was sometimes painted with elaborate designs.

Farther south, among the remaining Kwakiutl divisions, the Bella

27. *The old Haida village of Tanu, Queen Charlotte Islands, showing house frames and totem poles (taken about 1900). C. F. Newcombe photo.*

28. *Houses of the Alaskan Haida chief, at the village of Howkan, about the 1890s or early 1900s. The clapboard structure is a Europeanized version of the ancient house type; next to it stands the joined framework of a house of aboriginal type. Courtesy of Smithsonian Institution.*

29. *A Southern Kwakiutl (Gōasila) fishing camp on Cape Caution, show-ing the rough-and-ready type of houses set up at temporary sites. The same method of putting on the plank side, plainly shown here, was used in the old-style large winter houses, however. Courtesy of Smithsonian Institution.*

Coola, and the Nootka, houses were made according to a different structural plan. Heavy posts supported ridgepole and side plates, on which the roof planks were laid. So low was the slope of the two sides of the roof that some early sources described the houses as flat-roofed. Sometimes a double ridgepole was used. The siding of the house was erected separately, only secondarily tied into the frame-work; that is to say, pairs of poles were set up just outside the corner posts and roof plate, and planks were placed horizontally, slung on withes tied between each pair of poles (Figs. 29–32). These houses were particularly adapted to a custom of their owners, who commonly had house frames standing at various fishing stations, and would strip roof and siding off the house to take with them each time they moved. Elaborate crest designs were often painted on the house fronts. The Kwakiutl divisions, in recent times at least, copied the practice of the northern tribes in constructing plank-walled sleeping compartments inside the house.

30. *Southern Kwakiutl village at Salmon River.*

31. *Old picture of the Southern Kwakiutl village of Fort Rupert, showing houses with vertical (nailed) siding, and ancient type of Kwakiutl "totem poles." Courtesy of Smithsonian Institution.*

58

Among some of the Bella Coola and Kwakiutl divisions, and the Coast Tsimshian and possibly among the ancient Tlingit, if descriptive ancestral house names may be taken as evidence, a specialized variant form of house was made by groups living on very narrow strips of beach in the steep-walled fiords. These were pile dwellings, built partly or entirely over the water. Alexander Mackenzie describes in some detail the Bella Coola houses of this type that he saw on his historic trip in 1793. A modification of the pile dwelling, known, on the basis of archaeological evidence, to have been used by some Tsimshian, and according to traditions by certain Kwakiutl, was the house raised above high-tide level on a cribwork foundation of logs and poles. In brief, regardless of which basic house type they used, these northern

32. A Southern Kwakiutl village of the 1880s. The vertical planking on the house is one of the effects of the availability of iron nails. The boldly simplified carvings are typical of ancient Kwakiutl art, before the recent influence of the northern "totem pole" art.

33. A chief's house in a Bella Coola village (probably Kimsquit), probably near the end of the nineteenth or early part of the twentieth century. The house combines alien influences: the framed doorway and windows of European source; the false plates and nailed vertical planking are imitations of aboriginal custom. Note the difference on the rather ponderous carving of the crest-display pole from the vigorous old-style Kwakiutl carving and as well from the more stylized carving of the north. The gill net drying on the racks in the left foreground is of European commercial fishing type. Courtesy of Smithsonian Institution.

tribes had sufficient mechanical ingenuity to adapt their dwellings to any peculiar local need.

The Salish groups living around the Gulf of Georgia and Puget Sound, and their neighbors in northwest and western Washington, built houses of the same plan as the Kwakiutl, Bella Coola, and Nootka, with horizontal siding structurally separate from the house frame, but usually with shed, that is, one-pitch, roofs rather than gabled ones (Fig. 34). Wide raised shelves that served as beds and for storage ran along the walls. These houses were somewhat narrower than those of the gable-roof type, but some were tremendously long—a whole village or tribelet might occupy a single house of this kind. It

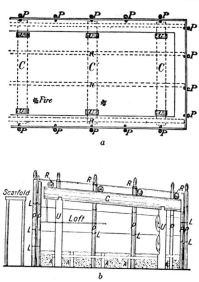

34. *Coast Salish shed-roof house:*
a, diagram showing construction;
b, section of house; C, crossbeams;
U, uprights; R, rafters; P, poles; L,
ropes made of cedar branches that
pass through holes in the boards and
are tied around the poles.

must be added that there was some overlapping of these two related house types: some Southern Kwakiutl and Southern Nootkans used the shed-roof type as well as the gabled roof; a few of the Gulf of Georgia Salish built both gabled-roof houses and those with roofs of a single slope.

At times, at camps and temporary stations, the Salish groups also built mat lodges like those of their interior cousins.

On the lower Columbia and along the Washington and Oregon coasts another house type prevailed. Although similar to those already described, it was a variant of the areal pattern of rectangular plank structure. A deep rectangular pit was dug and lined with vertically set planks. Corner posts and ridgepole posts supported long timbers on which the roof planks were laid to form a steep-sloping gabled roof, the eaves of which were just above the ground. Raised plank shelves like those in shed-roof houses were used as beds. The doorway was at one of the gable ends; one entered and descended a notched log ladder to the floor level. The Washington coast groups (except the Makah who built shed-roof houses), the Lower Chinook, and most Oregon coast groups had dwellings of this type. The Athapascan groups of southwest Oregon and the northwest corner of California built the same type of house, but with a pit only a foot or so deep, or without a pit, so that the house stood mostly above the ground.

The groups of the lower Klamath—Yurok, Karok, and Hupa—
built still another kind of house. In some respects it was more like the
structures of the extreme north of the area. The house had a deep
central pit, but the walls stood back away from it, leaving a step or
bench at ground level that served for storage space, as did a narrow
anteroom between the double front walls. Poor men might build a
house with a gabled roof, but a man of means and pride would have a
three-pitch roof. A round doorway, just big enough to squeeze
through, was cut through a big redwood plank on one side of the
gable end (Fig. 35).

There were few special structures in the area. The northwest
Californians built large rectangular sweathouses that served as men's
clubhouses. Certain features of these structures, as well as their use—
the exit tunnel that also served as a flue for the fireplace, their use as
a men's clubhouse, the direct fire-sweating rather than steam-sweating
—strangely enough recall both the *kashim* or men's house of the
western Eskimo and the *kiva* of the Pueblo tribes of the Southwest.
The groups around Puget Sound and some of their Gulf of Georgia

*35. Yurok houses of redwood planks. Note the double slope of the roofs
on the far side of both houses, which, with the slope nearest the camera,
formed the typical "three-pitch" roof of the lower Klamath. Courtesy
of A. L. Kroeber.*

relatives made small domed mat-covered sweatlodges, in which they took steam baths by sprinkling water on hot stones in typical Plateau fashion. In this, as in so many other traits, they reflected their close ties with their Interior Salish kin. Along the mainland shores of the Gulf of Georgia from Point Grey to Bute Inlet, semisubterranean lodges of pure interior type were known and occasionally constructed. Traditions of both Bella Coola and Tsimshian refer to similar structures as having been used by their ancestors long ago.

It has been remarked previously that the Indians of our area preferred water travel to any other method of transport. While, unlike the Polynesians, they did not make long voyages over the open sea, many of the northern groups were sufficiently competent mariners to cruise coastwise on voyages of several hundred miles. Kwakiutl and Haida raided the villages around Puget Sound sailing down Queen Charlotte Sound and the Gulf of Georgia in their huge war canoes.

In the north, Tlingit, Haida, Tsimshian, all the Kwakiutl divisions, and the Bella Coola used a type of canoe with high projecting bow and stern, a sharp vertical cutwater or forefoot, and a rounded counter (Fig. 36a). The projecting elements, which served to repel wave crests that would otherwise swamp the craft, were separate pieces, scarffed and fitted to the hull, and sewed tight with withes threaded through drilled holes. Elaborate designs were painted on the bows and, anciently, carved figures representing family crests were sometimes mounted fore and aft on the bowsprit-like projecting pieces. Some of the large canoes—for example the Haida dugouts made of the tremendous clean-grained red cedar of the Queen Charlotte Islands —were more than fifty feet long, and seven to eight feet in beam, and could carry a considerable quantity of cargo or a large number of warriors. While all the northern tribes made both large and small canoes of this style, the Haida canoe makers were especially esteemed for their craftsmanship, and the mainland groups sought to buy the Haida-built craft when the tribes assembled at the olachen-fishing grounds on the Nass River every spring. Gulf of Georgia and Puget Sound Salish constructed what was essentially a small low-sided variant of this type (Fig. 36c) for cruising their more sheltered waters.

The Nootka were also renowned canoe makers. Craft built by their experts were traded far and wide among their Salish neighbors, and even to the Chinook of the lower Columbia and the tribes of the central Oregon coast. The Nootka canoe differed from the northern

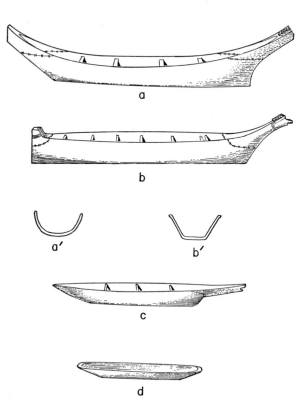

36. *Principal types of canoes on the Northwest Coast. All are shown with bow to right, stern to left: a, the "Northern" type; b, the Nootka type; a' and b' represent cross-sections, amidships, of the two types, and show important structural difference. Both these types of canoes were made in various sizes and proportions, that is, a seal-hunting canoe, intended to carry two or three men swiftly and soundlessly over the water, would have the same general outline, but be smaller and both relatively narrower and racier in line than one intended to carry larger quantities of freight or a war party; c, Coast Salish version of the Northern type, with low bow and stern, for travel on sheltered waters; d, small "shovelnose" canoe, used by many groups for river travel. These craft were built with both ends just alike.*

type in having a low vertical sternpost, and a graceful arc from the sharp-edged forefoot to the projecting prow piece (Fig. 36*b*). The bottom of the hull was flat and the sides were sheered, that is, flared outward to the gunwales, through a set of varying curves neatly calculated to ward off the seas instead of allowing them to come aboard. The graceful and practical lines of the Nootka canoe made it one of the finest seagoing vessels built by any primitive people. Some maritime historians believe that the flowing curve from forefoot to prow and the bold sheer of the bows of the Nootka craft inspired the New England designers of that queen of the seas, the American clipper ship, whose racy bow lines were nearly identical.

While dugout canoes were built on the lower Klamath, as in all

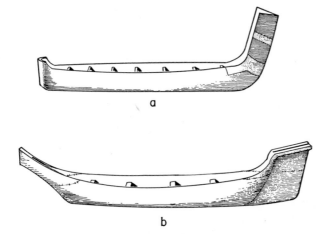

37. *Two ancient types of canoes, which have not been made for many years, but were seen by early travelers on the Coast and are recalled by elderly informants: a, war canoe formerly made by Southern Kwakiutl, and perhaps some neighboring Coast Salish. The high, wide bow piece (which must have been a separate piece, fastened to the hull at the lower margin of the wide white-painted stripe) served as a shield to warriors and paddlers when "hitting the beach" at an enemy village. Some early drawings (for example, those of the artist Paul Kane) show some canoes of this type with loopholes cut through the bow piece. b, Variant of the Northern type, with a deep boardlike bow which was usually elaborately painted, made probably chiefly by the Haida and traded to their neighbors. These craft may have been used principally for ceremonial occasions; they must have made a great deal of leeway in a cross wind.*

38. Lower Klamath dug-out canoe. Note the high steep ends (the stern differs from the bow only in having the seat carved on the inboard side) and rounded hull section that made this craft highly maneuverable in swift water, but cranky on the open sea. The chain painter is, of course, modern. Courtesy of A. L. Kroeber.

the rest of the area, a special local pattern was evolved. These vessels were primarily river craft, round-bottomed, straight-sided, with high freeboard, and with blunt, upturned ends that made them exceptionally maneuverable even in swift currents (Fig. 38). Nonfunctional yokelike pieces attached to the blunt prow and stern suggest atavistic survivals of the separate prow and stern pieces of the northern and Nootkan dugouts. Coast Yurok and their Athapascan-speaking neighbors immediately to the north put to sea in these craft, but for short trips only, for the canoes were better suited for river travel than for the deep sea.

The foregoing were the principal varieties of Northwest Coast canoes, but are far from completing the roster. A widely, if sporadically, distributed river canoe with round bottom, narrow, straight lines and bluntly pointed ends is usually called the "shovelnose" type.* Most of the Coast Salish made and used these craft for river travel, even the groups living on the seacoast who had Nootka- or northern-style canoes for use on salt water. In another part of the area, Lewis and Clark observed huge bluntly pointed dugouts, apparently over-sized shovelnose models, with large carved figures mounted at bow and stern, among the Chinook of the Columbia. Farther north, the Southern Kwakiutl and a few Nootka and Gulf of Georgia Salish who traded with Kwakiutl had canoes with a wide, entirely vertical prow piece, and short vertical stern like that of the Nootka type.† In the extreme north, the Yakutat Tlingit made a variant of the northern-

* Fig. 36d.   † Fig. 37a.

style canoe with an underwater projection, something like the ram of an old-fashioned dreadnought. This feature may have served to protect the hull from the salt-water "scum ice." The Yakutat and their Chilkat relatives knew and occasionally used Eskimo-style umiaks—large open vessels of hide stretched over slender ribs and wood framing.

Except in the extreme south of the area, all these canoes were propelled with paddles, usually with a lanceolate blade and cross or "crutch" handle. There were, of course, minor variations within the areal pattern. A Nootka sea hunter used a paddle that tapered to a very slender elongated tip, six or eight inches long, that was supposed to allow the water to run off the paddle blade quickly and quietly instead of letting the drops spatter noisily with each stroke to frighten the seal or sea otter. In the north, especially among the Haida, paddle blades were often elaborately painted with family crests. Southward, many Coast Salish and Chinookan groups had special paddles for river travel with deeply notched instead of pointed tips. The purpose of the notch was to enable the canoeman to brace his paddle against snags, roots, and boulders. In northwestern California, a combination pole and paddle, that is, a pole with a slightly widened, flattish end, proved most practicable for river use.

After a few years of European contacts, the Indians began to step masts in their seagoing canoes, and rig sails of heavily woven cedarbark mats or of canvas. Before that time, however, they knew nothing of sailing. Even after they learned to use sails, they could only sail with the wind well astern, for otherwise the keelless canoes made too much leeway, and could not possibly beat into the wind.

Other canoe appurtenances include bailers, of a variety of local forms, and neatly made tackle boxes shaped to fit snugly in the narrowed spaces at bow and stern.

Household furnishings consisted chiefly of articles made of wood or woven of cedarbark. Wooden boxes that served a host of purposes were made from Tlingit country to the coast of Washington. The Indian carpenter selected a suitable thin plank of red cedar, cut it to a width corresponding to the height desired for the box, then, after carefully measuring with a set of measuring sticks, cut three channels as wide as they were deep across the board, a good three-fourths or even more of the way through. Then, using his steaming technique for softening wood, he bent the board into a right angle at each cut

39. Kerfed and bent wooden boxes, Kwakiutl. The "hunters' boxes" tapered from top to bottom to permit stowage in bow or stern of a canoe, so the cuts were made slanting. Ordinary box boards were cut straight.

(Fig. 39). The two ends were scarfed and either pegged or sewed together with withes of spruce root. A rabbet was cut along one long edge of the board so that the bottom of the box could be fitted in snugly. Holes were drilled through sides and bottom, and dowel-like pegs were driven up hard to hold the bottom firmly in place. A box properly made in this fashion was absolutely watertight. It could be used as a cooking vessel by bringing water in it to a boil by dropping in a few red-hot stones, picked from the fire with wooden tongs. Fitted with lids, of the overlapping type in the north, or rabbetted among Southern Kwakiutl and Nootka, these boxes served for storage. In them were stowed all sorts of possessions: masks and ritual parapher-

40. End (above) and side (below) of carved Haida box, reported to have been used by a famous shaman for storing his professional kit. The carving on the end represents a Raven, that on the side appears to be a Beaver.

nalia, valuables, furs and clothing, trade blankets in historic times, and even the prized oils rendered from candlefish and from whale blubber. In the north, the usual crest designs were painted on these boxes, and the Haida often carved these designs into the box fronts and sides (Fig. 40). The northern storage boxes tended to be both squarer and squatter than those of Southern Kwakiutl and Nootka, who decorated their high narrow containers with tastefully spaced rows of fluting and inlays of sea-otter teeth and sea-snail opercula. There were many other uses for these boxes; they were made in different proportions according to their purpose. Very long narrow ones were slung from the rafters at ceremonials to serve as drums; small square boxes were made for water buckets. Quivers, babies' cradles, and trinket and tackle boxes were all made in the same technique (Fig. 41). The groups from the Chinook southward, who did not make these boxes with one-piece sides, made storage boxes by hollowing out big blocks of cedar or redwood and fitting snug lids to them.

Dishes were usually made in troughlike form, hollowed out of blocks of alder. The Kwakiutl and groups to the north of them often modified the basically simple dish shape into human or animal forms, especially in the case of the huge feast dishes (Figs. 42, 44–45).

While elaborately carved and painted backrests were made in

41. Kwakiutl cradle. The sides were kerfed and bent, like a wooden box. These cradles were padded with finely worked mats and shredded red cedarbark; the baby was lashed in securely so he could not fall out when the cradle was carried or suspended from a rope and swung. Cradles of chiefs' children were often elaborately carved or painted.

42. Kwakiutl wooden feast dishes.

the north, only the people of the lower Klamath made seats—simple but neatly finished redwood stools. Elsewhere people sat on the ground, or on the ubiquitous checkerwork mats of red cedarbark. These mats should really be considered furniture too: as has been remarked, they were used to sit on, as mattresses, and as tablecloths. The Salish groups and their neighbors to the south used mats of tules for the same purposes.

The Northwest Coast dress styles were very distinctive. As in almost all other aspects of the culture of the area, even most of the minor regional variation that occurred was within the limits of the basic patterns. Fitted or tailored garments were not used, except by the northern Tlingit divisions. The Chilkat division and perhaps their kinsmen who trekked over the mountains into the frigid interior often wore one-piece trousers-and-moccasins of buckskin, and fringed buckskin shirts trimmed with porcupine-quill embroidery, typical

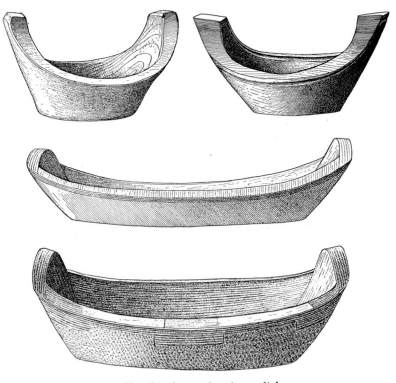

43. Kwakiutl wooden feast dishes.

44. Oil dishes of the Haida to hold grease in which food was dipped. These three specimens represent hair seals, not because that animal was a crest, but in reference to the fat rendered from hair seals and served in such vessels.

garb of Athapascan neighbors. Elsewhere, when the weather permitted, men went about nude—except for the Tlingit, whose breechcloth was a type of garment almost surely borrowed from the interior. Women wore one- or two-piece skirts of buckskin among Tlingit and Tsimshian, of shredded cedarbark among their neighbors to the south, and of strands of shredded maple bark or buckskin in northwestern California. Tlingit women wore their skirts over a rather shapeless buckskin slip, at least on cold days. In northwest California, a close-fitting, neatly made twined basketry cap was customarily worn by the women. On Puget Sound and among the Upper Chinook, women wore basketry caps of truncated conical form, identical with those of the Nez Percé and other Plateau groups. Throughout the area both sexes usually went barefoot, although nearly all the groups knew how to make rude moccasins for wear on the rare occasions when they traveled back into the mountains in winter. A number of early historic sources comment on the way in which the Indians walked about barefoot in the snow with no apparent discomfort. Whether this resistance to

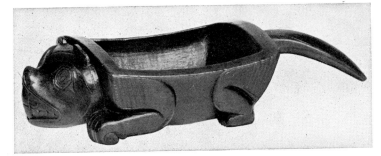

45. Feast dish representing a Beaver, probably of Tlingit manufacture. The striations on shoulders and buttocks symbolize beaver "work marks" on trees gnawed down by those animals.

cold was due to conditioning from childhood on, or to the oil-rich diet, or to a combination of both, is unknown. For rainy weather the Indians from the Columbia northward slipped on flaring conical capes, woven of shredded cedarbark, that covered them from neck to elbow but allowed considerable freedom of arm movement. Tsimshian and Tlingit relied principally on robes, and the Haida, Kwakiutl, and Nootka used rectangular rain capes of cedarbark matting. A tightly woven, wide-brimmed basketry rain hat (Fig. 46) completed the costume, although in cold weather a woven robe, twined-woven of shredded yellow cedarbark, might be worn under the rain cape. A robe of black bearskin, sea-otter pelts, marmot skins, or other warm fur was sometimes worn instead, especially by chiefs.

The woven robes of yellow cedarbark just mentioned were manufactured principally by the Nootkan and Kwakiutl groups, and perhaps by Coast Tsimshian, but were traded widely both to north and south. They were of a distinctive shape, being straight along the top and sides, with a curved lower edge that made the robe longer in the middle than on the sides. These garments were made of soft loosely twisted hanks of the inner bark of yellow cedar. To make a robe, the weaver hung the hanks of bark fiber, doubled over a cord suspended from a loom bar, and "twined" them together. In "twining," the wefts, or horizontal elements, were doubled, and each pair was crossed over about each suspended hank (or "warp" as the vertical elements in weaving are called) in turn, across the width of the blanket. The wefts were widely spaced, so that the surface texture was mainly that of the soft warps. In ordinary robes of this type the wefts were simply thin cords of tightly spun red cedarbark, but in better-quality products some wefts of mountain-goat wool were used. An added touch of luxury was given at times by sewing narrow strips of sea-otter fur along the borders of the robe.

A technically more elaborate robe, but one which in form, technique, and type of loom on which it was made was closely related to the cedarbark robe, was the so-called "Chilkat blanket" (Fig. 48). This English designation was given the garment because for many generations—perhaps the major part of the historic period—these robes have been woven only by Chilkat women. There are indications that formerly some other Tlingit divisions may have made them, how-

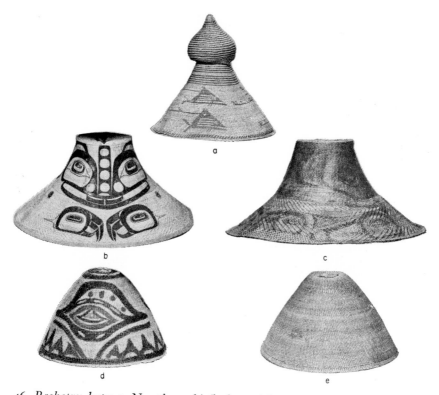

46. Basketry hats: a, Nootkan chief's hat with woven designs of whaling scenes; b, Kwakiutl type, with painted design; c, Tlingit style, with painted design; d–e, painted and plain types, Haida.

47. Kwakiutl woman in ancient-style cedarbark cape and robe.

ever, and that the technique may have been borrowed from the Tsimshian. According to one Chilkat tradition, the Tsimshian formerly made dancing aprons and half-leggings in the same technique. A Chilkat bride of a Tsimshian chief learned the art. At her death, a dance apron she had woven was sent to her home, where her relatives studied the weave, loosening and unraveling it bit by bit till they understood how it was done. They then began to make robes in the same fashion. This is of course not the only evidence of Tsimshian priority in the craft; some very old specimens, differing somewhat in style from recent Chilkat examples, have been observed among the heirlooms of Tsimshian chiefs. Also, as Lieutenant Emmons pointed out in his classic study of the craft, the Chilkat robes are decorated with the typically compact multi-element decorative patterns of the Tsimshian, whereas "dance shirts," a purely Chilkat development in the same technique, bear the more spacious and slightly more realistic Tlingit designs.

These robes, which are outstanding expressions of northern coast textile art, are woven by the women of yarn spun from mountain-goat wool (the warps are of goat wool with a core of yellow cedarbark twine; this latter material must of course be imported by the Chilkat). Men hunt the goats that provide the wool, make the "half-loom" on which the weaving is done (this is a loom with a single bar from which the warps are suspended with their lower ends free), make various measuring sticks and other devices, and paint the pattern boards from which the weaver copies her design. After months of spinning and dyeing her yarn, she is ready to set up her loom. First the warps are carefully measured and cut, so that their lower ends form the proper curve (in some specimens, the lower edge forms a shallow V rather than a true curve). Then she binds the warps together at the top with several rows of twined weaving, using a special variety of that technique. Her next step is carefully to measure the design panels of the pattern board, and to measure and count them off on the warps. Each lot of warps that will form a panel is tied into a bundle, and usually tucked into a container of dried mountain-goat or bear gut to keep it clean (Fig. 49). One of the unique features of

48. An excellent example of a finely woven Chilkat blanket. The strips of fur sewn on across the top were ordinarily sea-otter or mink.

49. A Chilkat weaver putting the finishing touches on a robe. Note the "half loom," from which the blanket is suspended at the top, the mountain-goat gut bags to keep the ends of the fringe clean, and the pattern-board on the weaver's right.

this weaving technique is that the robe is not woven as a single piece, but into separate panels which are joined together with sinew or wool-and-bark cord as the work progresses. These joints are concealed with a three-element false embroidery, which is also used to border each color area within the panel. Within the panel the weaving is done in a "twilled twining" technique; that is, the wefts seize two warps at a time, each row splitting the pairs of the previous one. The colors used are four: white, the natural color of the carefully washed wool; black, blue, and yellow. The three last-named were produced by soaking hemlock bark, copper, and lichen imported from the interior, respectively, in mordant solutions of urine, then dipping the yarns. The borders of the robe at sides and bottom are not woven, properly speaking, but are finished off in a sort of braiding technique. The long ends are left free to form a fringe, which is thickened by tying in additional strands.

The "dance shirt," a knee-length, unfitted tunic, usually sleeve-less, has been mentioned as a peculiarly Tlingit garment. It may be a replica of an ancient type of moosehide armor. Authorities are not in agreement as to whether it is itself an ancient form, or one recently developed by the Chilkat. The methods of weaving used are identi-cal with those used for the robe; it is simply woven on a higher and narrower loom. The dance aprons and leggings woven in the same technique are now quite rare. They have not been made for many years, perhaps since the Tsimshian abandoned the art.

It is interesting to note that the "Chilkat blanket" (and dancing shirt) is one of the very few ancient artistic products whose manu-facture is still carried on. After a brief period of experimenting with cheap, imported colored yarns, the Chilkat weavers returned to their aboriginal materials and methods, which they use to this day. The chief innovation is that commercial dyes, particularly for blue, are often used. The robes and shirts are rarely sold to tourists, however, for they are extremely expensive. The purchasers are traditionalist Tlingit, who buy them to have at hand for sentimental reasons, to display at feasts, and to be buried in.

There are a few museum specimens collected in early historic times, either from the Tsimshian or perhaps slightly farther south, in which weaves used and type of design vary from that of the more recent Chilkat robes. In two of these, both from the Tsimshian (Fig. 50), typical northern Northwest Coast designs are used, but in a different way from modern examples. The third well-known ex-ample, collected about 1800 somewhere along the coast, is distinctive because of its purely geometric patterns and the amazing variety of weaving techniques utilized (Fig. 51). Probably in former times there were a number of local varieties of this same basic type of textile in the northern part of our area.

The Salish groups along the shores of the Gulf of Georgia and the Straits of Juan de Fuca possessed three distinct textile weaving complexes. This is one of the very few fields in which they could demonstrate technologic superiority over their northern neighbors. They also used a greater variety of materials in their robes. Not only did they spin yarn of mountain-goat wool, but they kept a special breed of small woolly dogs which they sheared at intervals, just like domestic sheep. The fine down of ducks and geese, and, as well, the "downy" pappus of cattail reeds or of "fireweed," was mixed into and

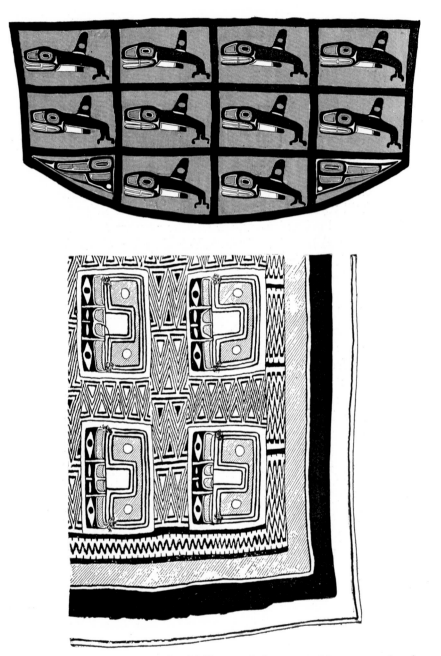

50. *Tsimshian weaving in the Chilkat technique: a, old goat-wool robe with Killer-whale design; b, geometric design on a shirt.*

51. Front and reverse of robe collected about 1800 in Tsimshian or Northern Kwakiutl territory. This specimen is interesting not only because of its geometric design, but because it is made with a variety of weaving techniques. Note that the left half of the (front) central panel is duplicated on the reverse side, whereas the color scheme of the right-hand panel is reversed, because of different weaves. The braided tassels on the front side are duplicated in a few old Chilkat blankets. Courtesy of Peabody Museum, Harvard University.

52. Coast Salish dog-wool blankets. The looms on which they were woven, and other appurtenances, such as the spindles with which the yarn was spun, can be found in a number of museums, but the only picture of the actual weaving process is this one painted by the artist Paul Kane. The small dog in the foreground is presumably one of the breed kept for their long woolly hair, with which the weaving was done. Photograph of painting by courtesy of the Royal Ontario Museum of Archaeology.

caught up with the long hanks of vegetal fibers and wool to make yarn. Yellow cedarbark was used little if at all by these groups. Some or all of these materials were beaten together with a special clay that cleansed them, carded with the fingers, and spun into a thick yarn on a long hand-twirled spindle with a large decorated spindle whorl of hardwood or bone that served as a flywheel to maintain an even tension on the yarn as it was spun.

One of the Salish weaving complexes—that mechanically most elaborate—involved the use of a "full," or two-bar, loom, with the single continuous warp stretched over two horizontal bars set one above the other in a frame and looped over a string (Fig. 52). When the blanket was finished, the cross string was cut and withdrawn and the two ends of the robe came apart. The robes were woven in a twilled checker (over two, under one) technique, like the rabbitskin robes of many Plateau and Great Basin Indians of the interior, from which they differ only in use of the loom. Probably the basic method is a heritage of the Plateau–Great Basin cultural ancestry of the Coast Salish.

The other principal blanketmaking technique, which was used for two quite distinct products, utilized simple twined weaving similar to that of the Kwakiutl-Nootka yellow cedarbark robes. We have little or no information on manufacturing procedures except for what may be deduced from study of the finished specimens. Probably the work was done on the same type of "half-loom" or suspended warp loom as was used by Kwakiutl and Nootkan weavers, and the makers of the northern Chilkat robes. The Salish twined-woven robes are typically rectangular in form, lacking the curved or shallowly pointed

53. *A robe of duck down, collected from the Makah, who learned to make such textiles from their Salish neighbors. The warps, which run horizontally as the specimen is shown (and was worn), are made of hanks of bark fiber into which quantities of down were caught. The widely spaced cedarbark wefts are not visible, being concealed by the down. The predominant color of the robe is the rich soft brown of mallard down, with a few strips of white; it is remarkably light in weight, but soft and warm. Courtesy of Smithsonian Institution.*

54. *A Coast Salish "nobility blanket," collected by Lieutenant Wilkes, U.S.N., on the lower Columbia River about 1841. The colors are chiefly native dyes: various tones of yellow and brown on a white ground, with a little black, blue, and red. The weave is plain twining; slanting design elements are formed by actually changing the direction of the weft elements from horizontal to the desired slope, and the undulating lines of the lower zone are formed by working the wefts in curves. The specimen could not possibly have been woven on the "full" or two-bar loom reported for the Coast Salish. The central panel, with the three broad stripes on the white ground, was apparently woven separately and sewed in along its sides, reminding one of the "panel weaving" of the Chilkat blanket. Courtesy of Smithsonian Institution.*

55. *(Opposite) A Salish robe of dog and mountain-goat wool, collected in the 1840s, which combines two very different weaves. The central (all white) portion is woven in the twilled checker technique, and could have been made on a two-bar loom. The sides are closely woven in a plain twining, with wefts slanted to produce diagonal lines, just as in the "nobility" robes. This specimen proves that the Salish utilized two distinct weaving complexes; the side strips are not mends, but integral parts of the original manufacture. Courtesy of Smithsonian Institution.*

84

lower edge of the yellow cedarbark robes and the Chilkat blankets. The two principal varieties of this Salish twined weaving were very different in appearance. One consisted of robes of wool and/or eiderdown warps with widely spaced cedarbark wefts (Fig. 53). The major difference between these and the yellow cedarbark robes of Nootka and Kwakiutl neighbors was in the materials; a secondary difference was that the twining was usually done transverse to the long dimension of the robe, rather than parallel to it as by Wakashan weavers. The other variety of twined weaving, the so-called "nobility" or "organized" robes, was one in which wefts were closely spaced, so that they, rather than the warps, formed the surface of the finished robe. Some of these blankets in museum collections, acquired around the middle of the nineteenth century, include yarns of European make obtained from traders, and some strands of native materials colored with non-native dyes, but most of the materials and dyes seem to be of Indian origin (Fig. 54). There are two characteristic features of the weaving that deserve mention: first, in a number of specimens a separately woven central design panel suggests relationship to the panel weaving typical of the Chilkat blanket; second,

56. Salish woven belts and pack straps (tumplines), collected about 1841. The techniques of weaving used are the same as those of the "nobility blankets." Courtesy of Smithsonian Institution.

diagonal lines in design were produced by slanting the wefts (pulling the warps to one side or the other) rather than by stopping a series of rows of a color one space shorter or one space longer than the preceding, as is ordinarily done in textiles and basketry. This is a most unique method of achieving the desired slanting effect. One might appraise the two major kinds of weaving as products of two distinct cultures, were it not that in a few specimens both techniques, twilled checker and simple twining, were sometimes incorporated in one and the same object (Fig. 55). Some belts and tumplines, collected from Coast Salish in the middle of the nineteenth century, were made with the same techniques as the "nobility blankets" (Fig. 56).

These Salish and Chilkat robes, and even the Kwakiutl-Nootka ones of yellow cedarbark that had a few strands of mountain-goat wool yarn woven in, were highly prized, and were traded widely along the coast, as far south as the Columbia River. Such luxury apparel was not worn daily, of course, but was reserved for festive occasions. Other articles of dress used by the three northernmost nations for special functions include dance aprons and knee-length leggings woven in the same technique as the Chilkat robes (Fig. 57). Dance aprons of buckskin and half-leggings, painted and, at times, ornamented with a little porcupine-quill embroidery, were found among the same northern groups (Fig. 58). They also used elaborate headgear composed of a maskette mounted on a headband, set with

57. *An old Chilkat dancing skirt. The design area, woven of mountain-goat wool, in Chilkat blanket style, is mounted on a buckskin backing. The jinglers on the fringe are mostly puffin beaks. The design in the woven area is Beaver. Courtesy of Smithsonian Institution.*

58. A very old Tsimshian dance legging (really a half legging, covering the shin down to the ankle). It is made of buckskin, with its design of porcupine-quill embroidery; the jinglers on the side are puffin beaks. Some leggings of this type were made with a design area woven of mountain-goat wool, then mounted on buckskin.

a   b   a'   b'

59. Chiefs' headdresses, consisting of forehead mask of wood with abalone-shell inlays, and a trailer of cloth (anciently of buckskin) covered with ermine skins. The forehead masks in concept, though not in style, are reminiscent of some Western Eskimo ceremonial regalia: a, representing a beaver, is from the Haida; b, representing a hawk, is Tsimshian; a' and b' are the backs of a and b.

88

sea-lion whiskers, and with streamers of ermine skins down the back (Fig. 59). Necklaces of various shells, especially the tusk-like dentalia regarded as highly valuable and dredged from a few offshore beds by the Nootka, were highly prized. In addition there were endless varieties of masks, carved helmets, and the turban-like rings of cedar-bark that were the insignia of the dancing societies, in use among all the tribes from Tlingit territory to the Olympic Peninsula. (The Salish of the Gulf of Georgia had fewer masks and less in general of the elaborate festive equipment than their neighbors to the northwest and west; those of Puget Sound had few or none of such luxury items.)

In historic times the "button blanket" became a popular garment for formal wear. This was either a trade blanket or other piece of heavy cloth to which many large pearl-shell buttons were sewn, the usual design being the outline of a family crest. Occasionally appliqué designs in red flannel were also sewn on trade blankets.

The Oregon and Californian participants in the areal culture had different kinds of equipment for festivals, but, as in the north, much of their paraphernalia consisted of articles deemed to have an intrinsic value. Thus, the dentalia shells prized by the more northerly peoples, on the lower Klamath attained a status approximating that of money among ourselves. Many-stranded necklaces of these shells were worn in the Californian dances. Huge beautifully flaked blades of red or black obsidian, another form of wealth, were carried by certain performers. Headdresses were wide bands of deerskin attached to which was another form of currency, the scarlet-feathered scalps of the pileated woodpecker. In fact, it has been said that in the festivals of the lower Klamath the individual dancers were of slight consequence— they were little more than mannequins who modeled and displayed the wealth and treasures of men of importance who sat by as spectators.

Personal ornament was somewhat varied, although ear pendants and nose pins (passed through a hole made in the nasal septum) were widely used. Clusters of dentalia were favored for wear in the ears; in historic times squares cut from the iridescent shell of the abalone, brought from the central California coast by white traders, came to have great vogue. Tlingit, Haida, Tsimshian, Haisla, and Heiltsuk women wore labrets—elliptical plugs of wood or bone, grooved around the edge like a pulley wheel. These were inserted in perforations through their lower lips. Young Kwakiutl and Nootka women wore tight-fitting anklets, and sometimes bracelets of bands of sea-otter fur, to improve their appearance. Face painting for every day was usually for cosmetic purposes—an all-over type for protection against sun, wind, and cold. Elaborate and multicolored designs were usual only on festive occasions, although among nearly all the tribes gay young dandies adorned themselves with showy patterns for no reason but vanity. In the northern half of the area, ceremonial face-painting patterns usually referred to the family's heraldic crests. Apparently only the Tsimshian had mirrors other than a basket or box of water or a tranquil pool. They made keystone-shaped mirrors of ground slate, with constrictions at the middle. By pouring a film of water on the smooth surface, a vain Tsimshian could contemplate his or her reflection. On serious ritual occasions, Kwakiutl, Bella Coola, and Nootka washed their hair and bathed, using stale urine as a detergent. Haida and Tlingit followed the same practice at times. Combs—some of them very ornate —were made for hairdressing, but were not worn (Fig. 60).

Some tattooing was practiced by most of the groups. The designs were often simple; the operation was casually performed. Crest designs, however, were tattooed on young persons of high rank in the north, particularly among the Haida, who used the most elaborate and extensive patterns and applied them on ceremonial occasions—that is, major potlatches. A high-ranking Haida man or woman was considered fully tattooed when the backs of the hands, both arms from wrist to shoulder, the chest, thighs, and lower legs, and upper surfaces of the feet bore crest designs. Sometimes the cheeks and back were

also decorated. At the southern end of the area, girls' chins were tattooed with broad vertical lines; no representative designs were used.

60. Wooden comb, Tlingit: the carving represents a bear sitting on its haunches, with a fish resting on its knees.

Along the lower Columbia and northward, newly born infants' heads were flattened by binding a padded board at an angle against the forehead. This produced a wide, flat form of deformation, sometimes referred to as the "Chinook" type, but also found among the Coast Salish. The Nootka and Kwakiutl used head pressers that produced an elongated, tapering head form, sometimes called the "Koskimo" type, after the Kwakiutl tribe who carried this type of deformation to its most extreme form. A third variety, known as the "Cowichan type," was found among the Gulf of Georgia Salish, and was more or less intermediate between the other two forms. The northernmost tribes did not practice head deformation.

The arms used in the area before the introduction of European muskets and cutlasses were: bows and arrows; spears, or rather pikes, handled like fixed bayonets, not thrown; slings; and a variety of clubs and daggers for attack at close quarters. The same type of bow, in fact the same bows, were used interchangeably for war and hunting. The typical bow was made of a short, rather heavy stave of yew or other hardwood. It was worked down to a cylindrical grip at the middle, which gave into wide arms that varied from flattish to triangular cross-section, and was strung with a heavy cord of twisted sinew. In the extreme north, among the Tlingit, the upriver Tsimshian, and the Bella Coola, and in the south, among the Chinook and the Oregon coast and northwest Californian tribes, sinew-backed bows—that is, bows whose elasticity was increased by fastening a layer of dried sinew to the back or outer side—were used by some hunters and warriors. This trait clearly reflects influence from neighboring groups of the more arid interior. In the humid climate of the Northwest Coast, a sinew-backed bow, despite its lighter weight and greater potential driving power, was not a very practical weapon. It needed special care to prevent the dampness from making the sinew backing, which should give the bow its extra springiness, soggy and unelastic. A few Tlingit used long straight bows with wooden string guards, modeled after a common northern Athapascan form. The bow, whether "self" or backed, was characteristically held in a horizontal position that probably was better adapted to use from a slim-waisted, cranky, sea hunter's canoe than was a vertical grip. The arrows used were commonly foreshafted, with ground bone or shell points. Chipped-flint projectile points were rare north of the Columbia, except for archaeological occurrences of relatively late prehistoric date around lower Puget Sound and the lower Fraser River, where interior influences extruded on the coast. The pikes used in warfare were usually short and heavy, tipped with bone or horn points or metal blades. In an emergency, of course, a man might defend himself with his fishing or his sealing harpoon, either of which would be a dangerous weapon in the hands of one accustomed to wielding it from boyhood. Before firearms were acquired in quantity, slings are said to have been used in warfare from Vancouver Island northward. A flexible basketry pocket made of spruce root was fitted with long cords of some strong fiber, such as that spun from nettle bast, and was used to throw good-sized beach pebbles. In war legends it is claimed that an expert could crack the hull of an attacking war canoe with a

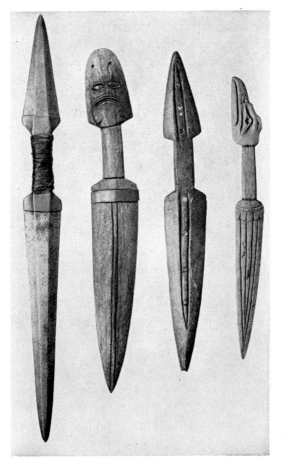

61. Double-pointed Tlingit fighting knives. The specimen on the left is of iron; the others are copies of the same type made of bone of whale.

62. Single-pointed Tlingit fighting knives, with elaborately decorated hafts.

sling-thrown cobble. Today, though the weapon has become a toy, lads develop sufficient accuracy to kill sitting birds and small animals with their slings. The first European explorers to visit the northern tribes found double-bladed iron daggers, with one long and one short blade on either side of the central grip, in common use (Figs. 61, 62). The fur traders had quantities of these daggers made by their ship's armorers for bartering purposes. Consequently, most of them now in museum collections are of late eighteenth- and early nineteenth-century workmanship. Many are of steel, but the basic design has an Iron Age appearance that fits well with the hypothesis of an eastern Siberian Iron Age source for Northwest Coast pre-European metal. These great daggers, with the short blade above the handle for back-hand passes, must have been very effective arms at close quarters. From Vancouver Island south to northwestern California heavy clubs carved from whale ribs were in vogue, and were duplicated in iron by machete-like knives (Fig. 63). Vicious-looking weapons, usually

93

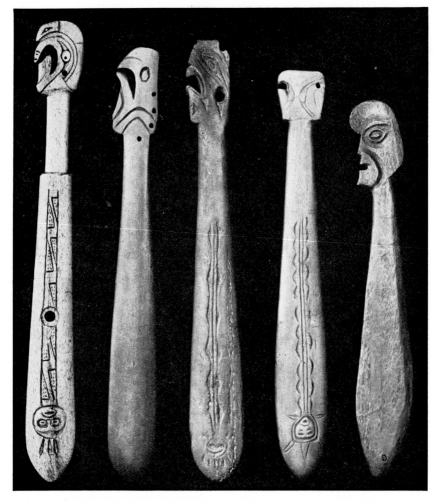

63. Sword-like warclubs of whalebone. These weapons were favored by Nootka and Kwakiutl warriors, and were often heirlooms, whose names and bloody histories were widely known.

like short-handled picks in form and commonly referred to as "slave killers," were found along most of the coast (Fig. 64).

Various kinds of armor were also used. Wooden helmets, often elaborately carved, with separate visors, also of wood, and cuirasses of tough withes twined together or of short flat rods joined by sewing with sinew or tough rawhide, were used by Tlingit, Haida, and Tsimshian warriors (Figs. 65, 66). Northwestern Californians also used armor of the twined-rod type. Cuirasses of heavy hide, such as elkskin, caribou, or moosehide, traded from the interior, were used by the northernmost groups. Farther south, warriors wrapped themselves with wide strips of elkhide so that they were covered from armpits to hips.

In the field of textile arts, the various types of robes woven of cedarbark, mountain-goat wool, and dog "wool" have been described, and the many uses served by mats and baskets have been noted. A survey of the present type is not the place for a detailed technological account of basket and mat making, but a summary of outstanding traits is of interest.

The red cedarbark mats were woven principally in a simple check-

64. Weapons of the "slave-killer" type. These implements, of hardwood, antler, bone, and even of stone, some one-piece, and some composite, were used by many Northwest Coast groups, and have even been found archaeologically in southwest Oregon. Their name in English comes from the fact that they were often used to dispatch slaves on ceremonious occasions.

65. *Mode of wearing Tlingit armor and arms, from a catalogue of a collection of specimens made in 1867–1868. The model was of the Chilkat division, to judge by his fringed buckskin shirt and trousers with attached moccasins. While the accuracy of old drawings is sometimes suspect, that of this one cannot be questioned, for the specimens shown— wooden helmet and visor, cuirass of slats of wood twined together, and the weapons—are in the collections of the Peabody Museum, Harvard University, and are just as shown, except that the designs carved on helmet and visor are in conventional Tlingit style rather than in the sketchy manner of the drawing. The eyeholes can just be seen as shallow notches cut into the upper rim of the visor.*

erwork, that is to say, with the wefts, or crossing elements, being brought over the warps in an over-one-under-one sequence. Each weft, of course, reversed the sequence of the previous one, going *under* the warp that the previous weft had crossed *over*, etc. Decorative patterns were made, especially on borders, by "twilled" checkerwork, which is like the twilled twining of the Chilkat blanket, in that each weft goes over two warps and under the next one or two. In addition, patterns were made by dyeing strips of bark and working them in. A black color was usually produced by burying strips of bark in mud; red, by boiling the bark in water along with a quantity of alder bark.

A variation in mat-making technique consisted in weaving mats in a diagonal (simple) checkerwork. To do this, strips of cedarbark were folded over at the middle so that one half lay at right angles to the

96

other end. Usually the folded strips were bound together by twining a light cord about them at the folds. The elements—in this case it is impossible to say which are warps and which are wefts—were interwoven in checker fashion, over one and under one. The point to making mats in this fashion was that new elements could be added in at the edges, where they would not create zones of weakness. While an expert could strip off very long pieces of bark from a tree, there is a limit to the length of a piece that a mat maker can handle conveniently. Therefore strips of bark were ordinarily cut to standard lengths. The length of the strips used as warps in an ordinary vertical-warp-horizontal-weft mat determined the length of the mat. Splicing in additional strips to lengthen the warps was unsatisfactory, for the strips would slip apart, unless they were knotted or twisted, which would create rough unsightly areas on the mat. By using the diagonal method, however, additional strips, caught in at the edge and doubled over to hold them in place, would not form a transverse zone of weakness at which the mat was likely to break in two. All the feast mats, some of them twenty, thirty, and more feet long, were woven in this way.

Strips of red cedarbark were woven together in the same simple checkerwork techniques to make baskets, also, from the Olympic Peninsula northward. Pieces of cedarbark were cut to a length that included the two sides and bottom of the basket to be woven. They were worked together in a simple checker weave at the midsections, forming a small mat with long loose ends at top and bottom and both sides. A light cord was ordinarily woven about the elements in a twining technique to hold them together, then they were all bent at right angles to the surface of the "mat," to form the "warps" of the sides of the baskets. Additional elements were then woven in, using the same checkerwork method, to form the sides.

Sometimes finely woven, flat wallet-like baskets were made of cedarbark in the diagonal checkerwork technique. The reason for making them this way was not to make them especially long, as in the case of the feast mats, but because the diagonal weave, like cloth cut on the bias, did not bulge and sag out of shape.

The best basketry on the coast was that made of thin segments of spruce root, or spruce root and cedarbark cordage woven in a twined technique. (This is the method in which the two parts of a doubled weft are crossed over each other each time they pass across a warp strand.) These baskets were so finely and closely woven that they held water. The elaborate ring hats of the Tlingit, Haida, and Tsimshian, and the Nootkan chiefs' hats decorated with whaling scenes, were all woven of these materials and in this way. The Northwest Coast, areally speaking, was the heartland of the development of twined weaving in North America. Technically, the groups at the extremes of the area—the Tlingit and Haida in the north, the Yurok and their close neighbors in the south—excelled in this craft, although the Nootkan women who wove the chiefs' hats, known from early historic times but not made for many a year, were not far behind in skill. (Only the Aleut, in all the continent, wove finer and tighter baskets, and Aleut culture, as will be shown, was related to that of the Northwest Coast.) However, most of the groups between the geographic extremes made twined basketry, except for the Coast Salish. These folk, in basketry as in so many other ways, continued an inland tradition. Their better baskets (some of them had learned to make twined baskets for special purposes) were made in the typical, and technically quite distinct, method of "coiling." Coiled basketry is, properly speaking, not a weaving technique at all, but consists in sewing together the rings of flat or ascending coils of rods or fibers. It

a

66. Various types of Tlingit body armor: a, of moose hide. The painted design appears to represent a Bear; b, probably of walrus hide, obtained from the Eskimo; c, of hardwood rods, twined together with strong cordage, and worn wrapped around the wearer's midsection. Courtesy of Smithsonian Institution.

is a method of making baskets which was especially characteristic of the Plateau, Great Basin, and Southwestern culture areas. In quite recent decades, some Nootkan groups who have had close contacts with Salish neighbors, through working alongside them in the Fraser River canneries and in the hop fields of the Puget Sound region, have learned to make this type of basketry, but they did not know the method in aboriginal times.

The well-made twined basketry was not left plain. Patterns were woven in, chiefly by a technique called "imbrication," which consists in laying flat strips of colored material over the weft elements to produce patterns. Angular, geometric designs were developed, for the most part, but a few of the better Tlingit and Haida basket makers were skillful enough to work in crest designs (Fig. 67).

Twining and coiling were both techniques that could be modified for special purposes. A competent weaver can not only make a basket

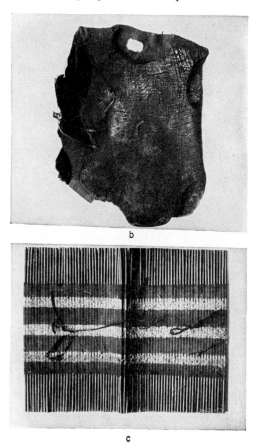

b

c

67. *Small-to-medium-sized Tlingit twined-spruce-root baskets. Note the fineness of weave. The decorative patterns are created by what is technically called "false embroidery" done in bleached and dyed grasses.*

that will be watertight, but, if the occasion demands, can also make an openwork one that will permit ventilation—for example, for the storage of dried salmon—in either technique. There were a number of special openwork techniques in common use also, along the coast, for making baskets for carrying shellfish, smelt or olachen, and the like, where drainage or aeration were desirable. Wrapped twining, in which one pliable weft element was given a round turn about not only each warp but also around a rigid weft laid across the warps, served to make quite sturdy yet open containers. Ordinary twined weaving, in which thick weft elements, widely spaced, were used, of course provided a simple openwork technique. A three-element checkerwork, in which the warps were crossed at each passage of the weft, was, so far as present information goes, peculiar to the Nootka, Southern Kwakiutl, and the Aleut, in all western North America.

Musical instruments consisted principally of percussion instruments: drums and rattles (Figs. 68–71). The tambourine drum, made by stretching a piece of rawhide over a narrow frame bent into circular form, was used only by Tlingit, Haida, and Tsimshian on the coast, though many groups of the interior, and Western Eskimo as well, used the instrument. The same three tribes of the northern coast, and all the groups to the south as far as, and including, those of Vancouver Island, made long narrow boxes of kerfed and bent cedar boards, which, slung from the roof and pounded with a sturdy fist wrapped in shredded cedarbark, boomed out the beat for dancers. Drumming with hardwood sticks on a long plank raised a few inches off the floor was another way of beating out time. The Chinook and southern Coast Salish reversed this: they used long poles, sometimes carved, and equipped with clusters of deer hoofs (so that they were also rattles), and thumped the ends against the roof boards overhead. Rattles were varied in form. Groups with considerable interior influence—Tlingit, Haida, Tsimshian, Coast Salish, Chinook, and northwest Californians—made considerable use of clusters of deer hoofs. The first three nations mentioned also used rings of withes

68. "Tambourine" drums. The drum on the right, with the design painted on the inside (where the drumming will not scuff the paint), is of a type old among Tlingit, Haida, and Tsimshian. The specimen on the left, from the Nootka, is a recent introduction among those people (probably latter half of the nineteenth century), brought in along with the gambling game known on the Coast as "lahal." The drumsticks represent two types used in the north; the straight stick type (lower right) should have a padded head of buckskin to keep the tip from cutting the rawhide drumhead and to give a more sonorous tone.

69. *Various rattles for musical accompaniment: a, of puffin beaks, Haida;*
b, follows the same form but uses teeth and amulets, Tlingit; c, of pecten
shells, Tlingit; and d, deer hooves on a stick, Tlingit. The two upper rattles,
a and b, are of a type widely used among Western Eskimo; c, represents a
type much more frequently used by Gulf of Georgia Salish than by the
Tlingit from whom this specimen was obtained; d, with variations, was an
interior type.

from which puffin beaks, animal teeth and claws, and the like were
suspended. Elaborately carved rattles of wood, the halves hollowed
out and fitted together, were common from Cape Flattery northward.
Rattles of mountain-sheep horn and of baleen, steamed and folded
over and fastened to wooden handles, were used by Kwakiutl and
Nootka shamans ("medicinemen"). Gulf of Georgia Salish danced
to the accompaniment of rattles made of clusters of large pecten shells
on a cord.

Whistles of wood, some with and some without reeds, were associated with the major ceremonials of the Nootka and Kwakiutl,

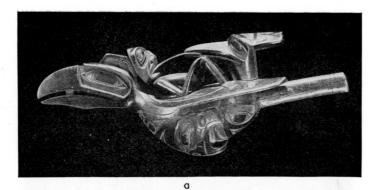

a

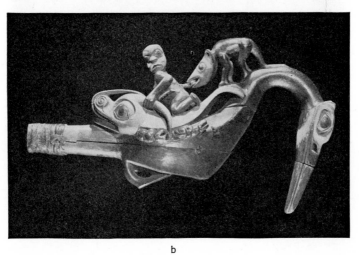

b

70. *"Chiefs' rattles": a, from the Haida, is an example of the "Raven rattle" often used by northern chiefs and some shamans to accompany songs on state occasions. The principal figure is that of a raven (the stylized face of a hawk is carved on the raven's underside). On the raven's back is a shamanistic scene, showing a spirit extracting disease from a sick person. The lower rattle (b), from the Tlingit, represents some large water bird, like a crane. On his back is shown a scene in which a person, apparently pursued by a wolf, escapes on the back of a friendly sea-monster; this is probably an episode in the origin myth of some clan. Rattles such as these were carved of two or more pieces of alder wood, carefully hollowed out for the "sounders" of pebbles, and fitted together.*

71. *Wooden rattles of various forms: a, represents a killer whale; b and d, hawks; c, represents a human skull; the motif of (e) is not certain. Globular forms like (d) and (e) were especially characteristic of the Haida; a, d, and e, Haida; b, Tlingit; c, Kwakiutl.*

where they represented the voices of supernatural beings, as did the bull-roarer, a flat stick whirled at the end of a string to make a booming noise. The northwestern Californians were the only peoples of the coast to have multi-toned instruments. They made simple little flutes, on which a man could tootle a plaintive tune, to amuse himself or to serenade a lady-love.

Gambling was a popular pastime among all the coastal groups except the Wakashan-speakers, aboriginally, and these folk became enthusiastic devotees of such games in late historic times. The most popular game was one or another form of "lahal," which consisted in guessing the relative positions of a marked and an unmarked stick or disk concealed in the hands of a member of the opposite "team," who sang lustily to confuse the guessers. Frequently two players on the same side each held a pair of these objects. The opponents had to guess the positions of all four pieces at once. Dice, made of sets of four beaver incisors, were tossed in a different type of game. Other contests, sometimes bet on and sometimes not, included wrestling, shooting arrows or throwing lances at marks, foot and canoe races, tugs-of-war, and variants of shinny. Youngsters played most of these games also, and like children the world over, many games of make-believe that were patterned on the activities of their parents. Myths were told both for education and entertainment. Of an evening, some old person would regale children and adults as well with the long, often humorous tales of the adventures and misadventures of such picaresque characters as Raven and Mink, or at times with the serious and important family traditions.

The cultivation of tobacco had a very peculiar distribution on the coast. The northwest Californians, probably most of the Oregon coast groups, and the Chinook sowed little plots of tobacco for smoking. Since the plant was widely used in aboriginal California, its occurrence along the lower Klamath is not surprising, although most California Indians did not cultivate it, but collected wild species. The reported use of a long-stemmed pipe with a stone bowl at right angles to the stem, among the Lower Chinook, hints most broadly at a trans-montane source for their tobacco and smoking habit, if they had not acquired the complex from the Californians before their ramified trade connections tapped sources so far east. However, the most mystifying and most isolated usage of tobacco was found among the Haida, where a plant, apparently a kind of tobacco, was sown and harvested and, mixed with lime, was chewed. Its cultivation was abandoned so early in historic times that we have only extremely meager information about it. Trade tobacco for smoking was obtained from white traders; its use became prevalent on the coast early in the fur-trade period.

The dog was the only animal domesticated on the coast. The dogs from which the Salish obtained their wool for weaving seem to have been a small, highly specialized breed; other dogs had no special attributes. Some hunters, particularly those who climbed the rugged mountains for mountain goat, trained their dogs to assist them in working the quarry within range.

FOUR

SOCIETY

THE STRUCTURE OF SOCIETY

Superficially, the Northwest Coast presents a picture of considerable diversity in social organization. Some groups were divided into social units based on matrilineal descent; that is, membership in the social divisions, and also the inheritance of social position and of worldly goods, came to each individual from his mother and her side of the family. Other groups had no formalized unilateral divisions (social divisions based like the above on relationships through one side of the family only), but nonetheless stressed patrilineality (kinship through one's father) in group membership and inheritance. Still others followed a bilateral reckoning of descent, with, at most, a slight preference for transmission of position and rights in the male line. As regards the relationships of these varying social units to each other, among some Northwest Coast Indians the basic social units—a group of relatives, their spouses and children, aligned according to any one of the three methods defined above—were politically autonomous. Among others, several of these basic social entities were formally united into what may be designated a "tribe." In a few parts of our area, a number of such tribes might be confederated into larger groupings for social and political purposes. In the northern half of the area, roughly speaking, a system of hereditary rank and chieftainship prevailed; in the south, possession of riches nominally gave one social ascendancy.

However, when these apparently varied patterns are analyzed, it becomes clear that fundamentally all derive from a few basic concepts and societal forms common to all the peoples of the Northwest Coast. The two basic principles of areal society are, first, that the fundamental social unit (aside from the biologic family consisting of a man, his wife, and their children) was the autonomous local group consisting of a *lineage* (a formalized, named group of relatives who trace descent to a common ancestor exclusively through one line—in our area, through the maternal line), or an *extended family* (a social division less rigidly formalized and defined, in which descent may be reckoned through either line, or both). As will be shown, it made no difference whether formal alliances were made with similar social divisions, for while such units united at times for purposes of common defense or for ceremonial ends, they never surrendered certain highly important rights. Second, social status, involving the so-called system of rank, derived neither from heredity alone, nor from wealth, but from a combination of the two.

As an introduction to a group-by-group survey of socio-political organization, it must be reemphasized that there were no true national entities among the Indians of the area. We have mentioned "the northern nations" and so on, but only after stating specifically that the term, in this usage, had no political significance, but referred only to linguistic units. That is to say, in these pages "the Tlingit nation" is a substitute for the clumsy phrase, "all the people of Tlingit speech." Terms like "Tlingit," "Nootka," "Yurok," and the rest are really linguistic designations, referring to all the independent political divisions whose members spoke those languages. The Indians themselves recognized that certain neighbors shared both the same language and the same culture, but felt no unity or common interest on that account.

The matrilineal type of organization just mentioned was found among the northernmost linguistic groups: Tlingit, Haida, Tsimshian, and Haisla. Among the Tlingit and Haida there were two major subdivisions to one of which every individual was assigned at birth, on the basis of the affiliation of his mother. Such twofold divisions of a national or tribal group are called "moieties," that is, halves. These divisions were "exogamic," to use a technical term which means that it was compulsory that each individual marry a person of the opposite division. Since membership was matrilineal, or through the mother, this meant that a man and his own children were inevitably in the opposite moieties. The Haida, for instance, were divided into two moieties, designated by the Indian terms for "Eagle" and "Raven." A man who was a member of the Eagle moiety had perforce to marry a woman of the Raven "side" (as the Indians express the term in English). The children of this couple automatically took membership, at birth, in the moiety of their mother; in other words, they had to belong to the Raven division. The same man's sisters' children, however, according to the same principle, of necessity belonged to *his* side—they were Eagles, and were considered to be, therefore, that much more closely related to him. The system is strictly comparable, though the mode of reckoning is reversed, to our own inheritance of surnames. Among ourselves, when Mr. W. T. Door marries Miss Sally Doe, their offspring will all take the surname Door (patrilinear inheritance instead of the matrilinear system of the Haida and their neighbors), no matter whether the Does are more socially prominent or not. The fundamental difference between our system and that of the Haida is that among us all the population is not divided into the Doors and the Does, each group with formalized rights and duties. The Haida and Tlingit no more disregarded paternity than we disregard maternal rights and relationships despite our insistence on transmission of the paternal surname only. A Haida's or a Tlingit's paternal relatives had both rights and duties of great importance that affected him (or her) all life long.

Members of the Tlingit and Haida moieties shared, as well as the moiety designation, the right to use certain "crests"—representations of animals or supernatural beings that were reputed to have assisted the legendary ancestors of the social division, or, in some cases, were said to have been the original ancestors. These crests are sometimes called "totems." Actually, they were more like the heraldic devices of European nobility, used for display to show one's ancestry. We shall return to this subject of crests, for they were one of the most distinctive features of native culture in the northern part of our area.

The next smaller unilateral social division is the "clan." By definition, a "clan" is a formal, named, exogamic, unilateral societal unit, whose members trace their relationship from a legendary common ancestor. Clans may exist with moieties (as subdivisions of them) or without them. The Tlingit moieties, for example, were subdivided into clans. The Tsimshian, on the other hand, had no moieties, but had three, and in some places four, clans.

Despite all this variation, however, all these matrilineal societies were built up around "lineages," the basic units. A "lineage" is once more a unilateral group, consisting, among our matrilineal northern nations, of a nucleus of men related maternally. That is to say, the Tlingit, Haida, Tsimshian, and Haisla lineages were composed of, for example, a group of brothers and maternal cousins, their sisters' sons, and the sons of the sisters of the second generation. The sisters themselves also were members of the group, but since as a rule they lived apart from it, being married to men of other lineages (and other clans and/or moieties, according to the rule of exogamy), they participated in its functions only occasionally. The wives of lineage members, belonging as they did to other lineages, had only limited participation in lineage affairs. The men's own children, of course, belonged to the lineages of their mothers.

This social unit, among the northern nations, was ordinarily politically independent. Even where, as among the Tsimshian, it had entered into formal alliances with other lineages, it retained its important economic possessions—fishing stations, hunting areas, berrying grounds—had its own house or houses, its own chiefs, and operated socially—and, as a rule, ceremonially—as an independent unit. It had its own crests, in addition to those to which it was entitled through clan and/or moiety membership. Innumerable ceremonial prerogatives were also vested in the lineage.

Haida social structure shows this basic lineage pattern most clearly. As has been remarked above, there were two great moieties among the Haida, the "Ravens" and the "Eagles," each with its set of crests and origin traditions. (Curiously enough, the raven itself was a crest of the Eagle moiety.) Each moiety consisted of a large number of named, localized segments, sometimes incorrectly referred to as clans. Each segment was a lineage, which held title to its lands of economic importance, occupied a separate village consisting of one or more houses, had its own chief and lesser chiefs. Each lineage waged war or made peace, staged ceremonials, and tended to its various affairs independently of any other.

Such a Haida lineage-village varied considerably in size. The shrinkage of population through the historic period, coupled with the tendency for survivors of decimated lineages to abandon their home villages and assemble at more populous centers, has obscured the picture somewhat, but early writers speak of villages of several hundred souls, as well as smaller ones consisting of one or two houses with forty or fifty inhabitants. It must be owned that these early figures are very rough estimates indeed, but we would probably not be far wrong if we used as an average thirty to forty persons per house. This would mean that there were anywhere from four to eight related adult males, about the same number of maternal nephews (sisters' sons), and a sprinkling of elderly widowed sisters or maternal aunts, in the average house. The other residents would be wives and children of the adult males of the lineage, plus a slave or two; these people of course were not lineage members. A large village, of eight, ten, or more houses, of course consisted of several sub-lineages, who still retained memory of their common relationship. The evidence indicates that in the course of time, if they prospered populationwise and economically, the sub-lineages tended to split off and become separate independent units, although retaining their feeling of relationship. For instance, the names of a number of traditionally related lineages on the Queen Charlotte Islands contain the term "Gitins." This word is meaningless in Haida, but it may contain the Tsimshian stem "Git-" or "Kit-," which means "people of." This linguistic hint is corroborated by the traditions of these lineages which agree that they are all descended from a single matrilineal family unit that came from the mainland later than the rest of the Haida, and may well have been of Tsimshian origin.

Each Haida village had a chief, who held that position by virtue of being the highest-ranking member of the lineage, and one or more house chiefs. The village chief (who was also the house chief of his own house) had a special title, the various versions of which translate either as "village master," "village owner," or "village mother." Each village was economically independent, owning its own village site, salmon streams, cod and halibut grounds, berrying and hunting tracts, and of course the camping sites that went with them.

The superficially similar structural pattern of Tlingit society differed slightly. There were two great moieties, named after the Raven and the Wolf. A slightly confusing feature was that, among the northern Tlingit, the Wolf division had many names and crests referring to the Eagle, and was commonly referred to as the Eagle moiety. In one of the southernmost groups, a small lineage called "Nexadi" ("Ne-hŭ-dee") also had many Eagle names and crests, and was regarded as a third division; that is to say, its members could marry into either Raven or Wolf groups. The origin of this little group is not known, but it is believed that it is probably of relatively recent alien source. Possibly an interior Athapascan or Niska lineage migrated to Tlingit territory and became Tlingit in language and culture. Many other Tlingit clans, according to their traditions, came originally from places outside Tlingit territory. However, these minor deviations in nomenclature and in accretion to the basic pattern cannot obscure the fact that the Tlingit had a true moiety system.

The first difference from the Haida pattern is to be found in the fact that the two moieties were divided into "clans." Some clans, like the Ganaxadi ("Ga-na-hŭ-dee"), the Kiksadi ("Kik-sŭ-dee"), and the Kagwantan, to mention a few of the larger ones, had a number of localized subdivisions, which were actually lineages exactly like those of the Haida. Although these local segments shared certain crests and traditions with the parent clan, they were politically and economically independent. There were also "clans," equated with the aforementioned units in the native mind, that consisted of a single local lineage group. Some of these were survivors of once larger units, whose other divisions had become extinct; others were clan subdivisions that, for one or another reason, had split off from the parent clan and, as it were, struck out on their own. In some cases traditions recall the original relationship; in others, that relationship has been suppressed or forgotten. These can be referred to as "clan-lineages."

Traditions of many of the clans indicate that their ancestors originally came from the south, near the mouth of the Skeena River, apparently prior to the arrival of the Coast Tsimshian, while others came from the interior, from what is now northern British Columbia. In connection with these traditions, it must be pointed out that while the Indians had no written records and had to rely on oral transmission of their clan and family histories, the traditions of all the groups from Vancouver Island northward are so specific and consistent—and, insofar as they can be checked, so correct—that there is little doubt that for the most part they are historically accurate, except for the occasional supernatural events that they recount, which we may regard as a sort of literary trimming.

The Tlingit were divided into fourteen named territorial divisions, or loosely confederated "tribes." Each tribe included one or more lineages (local segments of clans) of each of the two moieties. During the historic period, along with the decline of population, there has been a consistent trend toward consolidation of the "tribes" into unified villages. However, the evidence suggests that formerly each lineage had its own village, physically separate from those of the others of the tribe. Thus, one source reports that as late as 1880 there were eight villages of the Stikine tribe, five Kake villages, and so on. While the lineages of each tribe recognized certain mutual interests, there was no real unity. There was, for example, no tribal chief or over-all authority; each lineage had its own chief. Each lineage retained possession of its lands of economic importance, and exploited them individually. The lineages of a tribe might cooperate to make war, or for common defense, or they might not—they were under no compulsion to do so. The Indians insist, for example, that it was only certain of the Sitka lineages that attacked and razed the Russian fort in 1801, not the entire "tribe." Similarly, the lineage was the basic ceremonial unit. In other words, despite the nominal confederation of lineages in each region, Tlingit socio-political organization was quite like that of the Haida. The most important difference was that the Tlingit house-group, in cases where a lineage was of considerable size and had a number of houses each occupied by a sub-lineage, was somewhat more important than the comparable unit among the Haida. Traditions show that when a house-group prospered and grew, it tended to split off from the parent unit, move elsewhere, and become a new autonomous lineage.

The Coast Tsimshian and the Niska had a fourfold division, instead of the moiety or twofold division of Haida and Tlingit. Such divisions are sometimes referred to technically as "phratries," but we shall refer to them as "clans," since they were comparable to the major clans of Tlingit. These clans were named after the Eagle, the Raven, the Wolf, and the "Blackfish" (the killer whale and the black whale). The names of these divisions are interesting. Two of them, "Laxsgik" and "Laxgebu," mean "People (of the) Eagle" and "People (of the) Wolf," or "Eagle-people" and "Wolf-people," respectively. The names of the other two clans are meaningless in Tsimshian. The Raven clan is called "Qanada," a word probably derived from the name of the Tlingit clan "Ganaxadi" (and "Ganaxtedi"), which refers to a Tlingit place name and phrase, "People of (the village of) Ganax" ("Ganax" is also the name of a traditional Haida village site in the Queen Charlotte Islands). The designation of the "Blackfish" clan, "Gicpodwada" (gish-pod-wŭda), cannot yet be analyzed, except that the first syllable, "Gic-," is a variant of the previously mentioned Tsimshian "Git-," meaning "people" or "people of." The probable Tlingit (or Tlingit-Haida) origin of the name of the Tsimshian Raven clan points up the fact of the local shifts and migrations of population units back and forth across linguistic boundaries, especially frequent in the north. For example, one important Eagle clan among the Niska is known to have been of Tlingit origin; some ten or so generations back their ancestors, just before the epoch of European contacts, moved from Prince of Wales Island to the Nass, where they not only joined but adopted language and customs of the Niska. Several Tlingit clans can trace their genealogies to Queen Charlotte Islands Haida sources. Not only did some interior groups move out to the coast, but a few coast groups moved inland, up the Skeena, to join, and become Gitksan. The Tsimshian origin of one Haisla clan has been mentioned. Such population shifts of course must have been especially important in cultural transmission, and in leveling off the originally probably diverse culture patterns of the northern nations. To come back to the Coast Tsimshian and their social structure, each of the four clans was represented by a local segment, or lineage, according to our terminology, in each of the fourteen Coast Tsimshian "tribes." Nine tribes had their individual summer and fall fishing villages on the lower Skeena, their separate winter village along Metlakatla Passage near the modern city of Prince Rupert, and olachen-fishing sites on the lower Nass. Two tribes stayed the whole year around on the Skeena, just below the cañon. The other three coast tribes lived south of the Skeena, each in a separate village. The difference between these tribes and the so-called tribes of the Tlingit is that the localized segments of the clans, that is, the lineages, were more firmly integrated. While each lineage had its own chief and owned certain properties, the lineages of each tribe were ranked relative to each other, and the chief of the highest-ranking lineage was the recognized chief of the tribe. It appears that the tribe as a whole held certain properties, including the winter village site. In recent times, at least, each tribe acting as a unit has built the house of its chief, and considers the structure tribal property. It is not certain that this was customary anciently, however. The tribe as a whole usually participated in both ceremonials and warfare in former days.

The nine tribes who wintered along Metlakatla Pass seem to have been approaching a still more complex type of political organization, which was hastened but not quite crystallized by the historic incident of the establishment of a Hudson's Bay post at Port Simpson. The tribes moved their winter villages there, and formed a loose sort of confederacy, although the individual tribes never quite gave up their old autonomy.

The organization of the upriver Tsimshian, the Gitksan, was essentially like that of their coast-dwelling relatives, except that they had but three large clans, whose names are translated as Frog-Raven (equated with the coastal Raven clan), Wolf, and Fireweed (equated with the Blackfish division of the coast). A single localized clan, or clan-lineage, at the village of Kitwanga, named after the Eagle, had the right to use names and crests referring to that bird. Tradition relates that the ancestors of this group came originally from the Nass River.

The Kwakiutl-speaking Haisla of Douglas and Gardner canals were the southernmost people on the coast to have a matrilineal type of social organization. There is no doubt but that these folk acquired their social system from their Tsimshian neighbors. In fact certain clans or clan-lineages are traditionally reputed to have been of Tsimshian origin, and many Haisla have Tsimshian blood from recent intermarriages. There were two Haisla tribes, with principal winter villages at Kitamat at the head of Douglas Canal, and at Kitlope, up Gardner Canal, respectively. (As has been noted, both names are Tsimshian, not in the Haisla dialect of Kwakiutl at all. "Kitamat," for instance, is said to mean in Tsimshian, "People-of-the-snowy-place.") There are said to have been a total of six clans (including one clan-lineage), each with its own crests and traditions: Eagle, Beaver, Raven, Crow (extinct for some time), Blackfish, and Salmon (a clan-lineage, found only at Kitamat). The lineages of each of these units had their own chiefs, houses, and fishing grounds.

The various possessions that have been mentioned as being vested in all the northern lineages: crests, houses, and lands, were not the only forms of lineage-held properties. Personal names, songs and dances for ceremonial occasions, and ceremonies or specific parts of ceremonies were also so regarded. It is true that where clans occurred, there were certain crests and other prerogatives that were considered to be clan property. However, these things were handled in the same way that the lineage possessions were. The basic concept was that all the members of the unit shared in the joint right to these prerogatives, as they are often termed, but that the chief of the lineage was the custodian both of the intangible rights and of the lands and material possessions. The lineage chief was in this respect similar to the executor, in our own culture, of a large estate who manages its various enterprises for the heirs. It was the chief who decided when the group should move from the winter village to their fishing station and commence work on the weirs and traps. It was he who decided that a mask representing a certain hereditary crest should be worn by a dancer in a ceremonial, and that certain lineage-owned songs should be sung. The chief, once more, was the one who formally bestowed hereditary names referring to lineage crests on young members of the group. All these varieties of possessions, material and intangible alike, constituted the wealth of the social group. The better the use their chief made of these riches, the more was the well-being and prestige of the group enhanced.

South of the region in which matrilineal organizations prevailed, from the Heiltsuk to the Nootka and the Gulf of Georgia Salish, the formal social structure differed. There were no moieties, clans, or lineages. Descent was reckoned bilaterally, with only a slight preference for the male line. It is true that most Heiltsuk groups (both Xaihais and Bella Bella) had divisions named after the Eagle, Raven, Blackfish, and Wolf, which they themselves equated with the Tsimshian clans. However, they had neither a strict rule of descent determining affiliation in these groups, nor of exogamy, two concepts which are indispensable to true matrilinear organization. A man and his wife might assign their first child to the father's so-called "clan," the next to the mother's, if she were of a different "clan," depending on the names and rights they wanted each child to share—a procedure that would have scandalized any right-thinking Tlingit, Haida, or Tsimshian. Basically, these people, like their Southern Kwakiutl, Nootka, and Gulf of Georgia Salish neighbors, were organized into

extended families. Each of these extended families had a series of land
holdings that included all-important economic resources—salmon- and
herring-fishing grounds, hunting tracts, shellfish and berry tracts, etc.
—and a host of ritual and intangible possessions: the right to use certain crests (not associated with clans), to perform certain dances and
ceremonies, to use certain masks, to bear certain names, and many
more. The chief of the extended family, like the chief of the northern
lineage, was the custodian of all these rights. Membership in the extended family was inherited from one's parents. Although, when
the parents stemmed from different local groups, a person was considered more closely allied to his father's side, he retained some
claim to rights in the maternal line. On the marriage of his daughter,
or the daughter of any important member of the extended family, it
was not uncommon for a chief to bestow certain of the family prerogatives on the groom, thus in effect transmitting them to the bride's
children when born.

The political units developed from this basic local group-extended
family pattern varied considerably. Some groups, like the Xaihais, a
few of the Southern Kwakiutl, the Central and probably the Southern
Nootka, and most of the Gulf of Georgia people, never developed
more complex structures. On the other hand, just before or shortly
after the dawn of the historic period, four Bella Bella groups, certain
of which may have actually been tribes consisting of several local
units, joined forces, establishing a common winter village at a place
called Noluh. The Bella Coola likewise had several tribal winter villages at each of which a number of otherwise independent local groups
assembled. Data on the Wikeno are fragmentary, but it seems likely
that there was at least one tribal grouping on the Inlet, and two among
the Wikeno Lake groups. Many Southern Kwakiutl divisions and
Northern Nootkans also united into tribes, as did the Salish Homalco-
Klahuse-Slaiamun divisions of the Gulf of Georgia. The hallmark of
these tribal unions was the sharing of a winter village site, an established seriation or order of rank for the chiefs of the constituent local
groups, and frequent, though not invariable, joint participation in
ceremonials and in war.

A few groups went even further, creating confederacies. Some
Northern Nootkan tribes, particularly those residing about a large inlet, assembled at a common summer village, established a fixed order of
rank for all their chiefs, participated jointly in rituals (sometimes the

highest-ranking of the chiefs represented the whole confederacy), and, on occasion at least, presented a solid front in war. Such a unit might have as many as thirty houses at their confederated summer site, and even well along in the historic period might include more than a thousand people. The four Southern Kwakiutl tribes holding the coast from Neweetee territory to the Nimkish River—the Walas Kwagiutl, the Kwexa, the Kwagiutl or Guetela, and the Qomkutis, and for a time the Matilpe—like the nine Coast Tsimshian tribes, formed a confederacy as the result of a historic stimulus: the establishment by the Hudson's Bay Company of a trading post, Fort Rupert, in 1849. Their difficulties in attempting to integrate their tribal system into a smooth-running confederacy will be described below.

The Puget Sound peoples and those of the lower Columbia were culturally disrupted so early by white settlement that much information on their social organization is irretrievably lost. However, it is fairly certain that the autonomous local group, consisting of an extended family, was the prevailing form. It is not clear whether they accented patrilineality in determining group membership and inheritance, or whether they permitted as much flexibility as did their bilaterally reckoning northern relatives and neighbors, although there are suggestions that they stressed kinship through the male line, as in western Washington.

In northwestern California the extended families were smaller. The tendency was for them to split up into small units of close kin. Several such groups, some vaguely related, others unrelated (or the fact of relationship forgotten), might share a village site. But each family group had its own lands, its own head man, and acted independently of the rest. Parts or all of a village might cooperate in ceremonies, particularly in the major festivals, but that was simply because no one family had either the personnel or resources to handle the performance unaided. Warfare likewise reduced itself to interfamily feuds; unrelated neighbors were careful to avoid involvement.

Northwest Coast society as a whole was distinctive in western North America because it graded individuals into a series of relatively higher or lower statuses. Examples of these ranked statuses were the chiefs, the nobles, the commoners, and the slaves. This phenomenon has been appraised superficially as indicative of the existence of a class or caste system which, to the Western mind, immediately suggests rigid sharply separated social strata within each society. Such

an interpretation does not conform with the facts, except for the
slaves, who formed, at least occasionally, a quite distinct societal unit.
Actually, the members of each group occupied a series of social positions that were graded in minute steps from high to low. Within each
graded series it is impossible to mark off a fixed point separating noble
from commoner. Furthermore, despite the avowed rigidity of the
system, it was possible for a person to modify his own status slightly,
for better or for worse, and to improve or worsen that of his children
(or that of his maternal nephews in the case of the northern matrilineal societies).

We may begin by examining the nature of the graded series of
statuses just mentioned. It has already been pointed out that the basic
social unit, the autonomous local group, invariably centered around
a group of blood relatives, either a lineage or two or more sub-
lineages, or an extended family. The chief or head of this unit was
normally the oldest member of the group descended in the most direct
line from the lineage ancestor or ancestress. It is true that among some
groups, particularly the Coast Salish (Bella Coola conformed with the
practices of their linguistic congeners in this respect, rather than with
those of their Kwakiutl neighbors), there was some variation allowed,
so that a more able junior relative might be awarded the chieftainship. Nonetheless, the native theory still held that the chief should
stand in the relationship of the eldest to the other members of his
group. The chief's younger brothers were his presumptive heirs and
therefore next to him in rank. The formal rank of all the other members of the lineage or the related lineages was reckoned on the same
basis—that of kinship to the direct chiefly line. The lowest-ranking
individual, in other words the lowest commoner, was the most distant
relative who was still counted as a kinsman by the members of the
group.

As will be noted below, while social status was derived in this
fashion from genealogical relationships, it was in a sense not automatically acquired at birth, but had to be formally assumed; that is
to say, to take one's proper place in the group a person had to take
or be given the proper name or title from the family stock of these
honorifics. At a ceremonial occasion he had to present evidence of
his right to use lineage or extended family crests and similar prerogatives on the same sort of formal occasions and so on. The names
and titles that he might take, the crests he might display at once

demonstrated the particular level of his rank in society and depended on the nearness of his blood kinship to the direct line of descent from the group ancestor or ancestress. Even the lowest-ranking commoner was entitled to certain categories of names that belonged to the group, and was entitled to participate in the all-important ceremonial affairs of the group. It is obvious, therefore, that within every social unit there was an unbroken, graded series of statuses from high to low. Informants have no hesitation in saying that "so-and-so was a noble," or that "so-and-so was a commoner"; but they find it difficult to define precise status for those who fit in between these two extremes.

Even among the groups on Vancouver Island and northward, among whom the system of graded ranking was most elaborated and theoretically most rigid, an individual could modify his social standing. A man of quite low rank who was a skillful canoe maker or mask carver or a bold warrior often became so valuable a member of the group and so esteemed by the chief that he might be given certain prerogatives beyond those to which he would have been entitled simply by reason of birth. Such privileges might include a higher-ranking name, a title of "war chief" if the man were a warrior, the right to use a special crest, or exclusive rights to some good fishing spot. At times, instead of giving these rewards to the individual himself, the chief might give them to him for his children or maternal heirs, as the case may be, or bestow them directly upon his heirs. Contrariwise, a man who fell into disfavor could expect only the barest minimum as his share of the honors and economic benefits of the group. The Coast Salish, including the isolated Bella Coola, permitted a great deal of such shifting up and down the social scale, according to an individual's outstanding qualities or lack of them.

The importance of properties in real and material wealth and in intangibles, such as the right to use names and crests, has been mentioned several times. In the preceding paragraphs the significance of heredity, genealogically speaking, in fixing a man's social position has been stressed, but it is necessary to bring the intimate connection between heredity and wealth into proper perspective. In the final analysis, social status on the Northwest Coast did not depend entirely either on heredity or on wealth, but on the interrelationship between the two. The chief, by virtue of his noble birth, was the custodian of the lineage wealth and was entitled to use and manipulate these properties, particularly the ceremonial ones. Therefore in a sense he was the richest individual of the group. His noble juniors were also empowered to utilize certain of the group properties, but not those of the very highest rank or esteem. Low-ranking members were by birth entitled only to very minor rights from among the family properties.

Of course the manifestations of this concept—of rank as stemming from the interaction of heredity and wealth—were not identical throughout the entire area, although the basic forces were the same. The preceding discussion applies most specifically to the Indian communities from Yakutat Bay to Nootka territory. The Coast Salish, except for a few Gulf of Georgia groups strongly influenced by Kwakiutl neighbors, possessed far less wealth in the form of titles, ceremonial privileges, and crests to use—consequently they had fewer formal means of indicating each person's social position. There seems to have been less differentiation of status—less of a spread, as it were, between high and low. Nonetheless the chief's prestige, augmented or not by personality factors, stemmed from his custodianship of group properties. Along the lower Columbia, early historical sources contain descriptions of Chinookan chiefs of considerable power, and what seems to have been a somewhat overdrawn picture of variation of social rank. Certain chiefs were undoubtedly very powerful, but apparently their authority was basically the same as that of the Coast Salish chiefs, exceptional powers deriving from two factors: first, a strong personality on the part of the chief himself, and second, a large and unusually closely knit lineage standing solidly behind him. In northwestern California, with the smaller social nuclei, we get the impression of a greater accent on individual ability. Yet in the final analysis, the Yurok or Karok "rich man" or head of the little family group attained his position because he had inherited custodianship of the family's treasures of white deerskins, great flint blades, and strings of dentalia.

It would appear on the face of the information available that the bases of the Northwest Coast system of rank statuses should have been fairly clear to investigators. Nonetheless one finds many contradictory, ambiguous statements in the literature. The principal reason for this seems to be that developments within the historical period superficially modified the system. Two things happened during the nineteenth century. One of these, which had its beginning in the sea-otter fur trade, was that varieties of material wealth became available from a source external to the culture. Brass and iron jewelry, abalone shells from California, blankets, firearms and steel tools, all prized possessions, could be obtained at the cost of little effort by anyone who wanted to devote some time to hunting sea otter and, later, by trapping fur-bearing animals on land or signing on a fur-sealing schooner. Some groups—the Chilkat, the Stikine, the Coast Tsimshian and the Fort Rupert Kwakiutl, who were in a position to control trade with interior fur hunters or coast groups remote from the trading posts— netted tremendous profits by acting as middlemen in the fur trade. Hence great amounts of material wealth, such as was necessary for the prestige-giving ceremonials, was suddenly made available. More numerous and more spectacular ceremonials were, therefore, given in this period than ever before. The second factor was the sharp decline in native population brought about primarily by the introduction of European diseases, and secondarily by the increased efficiency of native warfare resulting from the introduction of firearms. It eventually happened that among some dwindling groups there were more noble titles and crests available than there were people to bear them. Consequently, a man of low rank—one who was only remotely connected with the chiefly line of descent—might nevertheless find himself the heir presumptive to the chief's position or, as often was the case, one of two or three equally distantly related survivors. Were he an industrious fur hunter, he could assemble enough material riches to stage a great ritual at which he would announce his right to the high rank, titles, and crests—a situation that would have been completely impossible in the aboriginal era when the population was in a state of equilibrium. Quite as frequently, when there were several commoner survivors, they engaged in the bitterest sort of competition for the high statuses. Therefore, during the past century there were innumerable prestige-claiming ceremonies, many more than would have been performed in prehistoric times, and a great many of them staged by people who anciently never could have performed them at all. The extent of the social gap between these *nouveau riche* claimants to high positions and unambitious commoners was falsely accentuated out of all proportion.

It has been remarked that slaves, as a group, came close to forming a distinct social stratum. Slaves on the Northwest Coast were primarily war captives, although in northwestern California a debtor could be reduced to slavery. A slave was a chattel in every sense, with no rights whatsoever. He was considered to be a valuable possession, not so much because his economic activities contributed to the riches of the group (although ordinarily he would be made to work and do menial chores), but because ownership of a slave indicated either success at war on the part of his owner or control of sufficient material wealth to purchase these unfortunates. In individual cases slaves might be treated well, but on their master's death they were likely to be killed. The sacrifice of a slave was interpreted to mean that the owner was so rich and powerful that he could unconcernedly destroy a valuable possession. Tlingit chiefs frequently crushed slaves to death under the enormous house posts set up at a ceremonial house-building. On the arrival of a visiting chief, Kwakiutl sometimes killed slaves on the beach in order to use the bodies "as rollers for the chief's canoe."

The enslavement of a relative was felt to be a disgrace to his entire lineage, so that his family made every effort to secure his freedom—usually by paying a ransom for him. Consequently, many war captives were sooner or later freed by their kinsmen; after a performance of ceremonials to cleanse them of the dishonor, they resumed their normal status in society. Ordinarily, therefore, it was only slaves who had been captured and carried a great distance from their homes—Puget Sound Indians enslaved by the Haida, or northern Californian natives captured and traded at The Dalles and down the Columbia to the coast—who had little chance of ultimate freedom. Slaves taken from nearby groups were usually either killed by the captors or ransomed by their kin. Hence, while slavery did involve a distinct separation from the rest of society, it was, in many cases at least, merely a temporary condition.

THE POTLATCH

The ceremonial at which the various prerogatives intimately associated with social status were assumed was called in Chinook jargon, which was the *lingua franca* of the Northwest Coast, the "potlatch." Each major cultural division, from the Tlingit to the Lower Chinook, had its own variations in procedure and detail of this performance, but the function was everywhere the same. The potlatch brought to expression basic principles involved in social status and also served as a major force for social integration. As has been stated, each individual in the social unit was born with an inherent right to use group properties of major or minor importance, but he could not exercise these rights—in other words, assume his proper status—until his title to them had been formally announced and validated. This formal announcement and public validation was accomplished during and by the potlatch. The heir presumptive to a chieftainship would be presented formally to a group of guests at such an affair. His relationship to the incumbent chief would be explained and he would be given a name or the right to use some crest specifically related to the position he would eventually occupy. Under some circumstances a man might, in the same manner, present himself as a presumptive heir. The guests who heard these claims announced, and recognized their validity, were regarded as witnesses to the proceedings. As such, they were rewarded and their subsequent good will was insured by giving them feasts and gifts. While at times the demonstration of privileges or the giving away of material goods might appear to overshadow the essential announcement and validation of rights and status, this last-named function was the essence and basic goal of the whole performance.

The contribution of the potlatch to group solidarity was achieved in various ways. The proper giver of the potlatch was, of course, the chief of the local group, although in some instances where progress had been made toward tribal solidarity, the ranking chief of the tribe might give the affair. The chief performed this function as custodian of the family's wealth in goods and intangibles. (When a tribal chief was the host, he used only his own lineage crests.) He was the principal host, but, in point of fact, all the members of the family assisted and joined him as hosts. The guests, who provided the necessary validation of the claims made, were necessarily outsiders. They might be from another group of the same tribe, or they might come from an entirely separate and independent community. Furthermore, since gifts and material goods—which in historic times were synonymous with trade articles like blankets, guns, and other European imports, as well as cash—were essential, all the members of the host group contributed to make the total quantity available for distribution to the guests as large as possible. The host group also cooperated with their chief in assembling foods for the feasts, in providing dancers and singers for the crest displays, and in innumerable other ways. In fine, every member of the host group participated actively and thus had many opportunities to demonstrate his membership in the group and to share the prestige acquired from the ostentatious display. Another contributing factor was the fact that not only was the heir presumptive given titles and other honors, but other members of the group had rights to the public bestowal of whatever family rights to which they might be entitled. Children of individuals of intermediate and low rank alike would be given names from the family stock or have their ears pierced at the potlatch, or in one way or another would be presented as members of the group. Thus, in a variety of ways, the institution was a group affair that affirmed or reaffirmed the group affiliation of each of its members.

The basic pattern was embroidered on and elaborated in various ways by each of the northern divisions.

The Tlingit viewed the potlatch as a cycle of rituals to mourn the death of a chief. It was not a single performance, but one that might take several years to carry to completion. It began with the reward to the group who had conducted the mortuary rites for the chief. These people always had to be of the opposite moiety from that of the deceased, that is, if the chief had been a Raven, a group from the Wolf side would take care of the body and bury it. In theory at least, this group should belong to the same lineage as the dead chief's father. In any case they were formally invited to a potlatch at which the new chief, the heir to the deceased, was presented. His rights to the position were explained and the origins of the various proper ties were recounted. For serving as witnesses, and for coming, as they said, "to console the (new) chief for his loss," they were given presents. At the same time, the chief who had been designated to take charge of the funerary proceedings was "paid." Subsequently, until the cycle was completed, the same people were summoned on various occasions: to rebuild the house of the new chief, and to raise a mortuary column in memory of his predecessor. Specifically, they were called upon to perform these tasks: to carve the mortuary column, to cut and carve the house posts, etc., so that some of the gifts were given to them in payment for their efforts, and some were given them simply as gifts.

The Tsimshian potlatch was essentially the same, although the overt expression of its purpose is sometimes stated as being that of inheritance—that is, the announcement of and validation of the position of the new chief—rather than to stress the mourning function as did the Tlingit. Actually the potlatches of both peoples were essentially the same, serving at the same time to honor and commemorate the departed chief and to establish his heir officially in his place. The Haida, as will be brought out, likewise staged such affairs.

The Haida, according to available published sources, seem to have given potlatches most frequently to establish the position of a younger person as the heir presumptive. That is to say, a potlatch might be given in a child's honor by his parents before he went to live with his maternal uncle, whose status and rights he would eventually inherit. Although the child's father appeared to function as a host, the actual hosts were the mother and her lineage, who provided the property—both the ritual prerogatives bestowed and displayed and the material goods distributed as gifts. The father's lineage were the guests. Eventually, on the death of the maternal uncle, the heir gave a potlatch in the house which he was entitled to inherit, using the prerogatives and wealth of his own lineage. These combination memorial–status-assuming affairs were probably the major ones given by the Haida, as they were amongst their Tlingit and Tsimshian neighbors.

Among the Kwakiutl, Bella Coola, and Nootka, potlatches were often given, like those of the Haida, to establish a child or youth as the heir presumptive. In addition, these three peoples very often combined the potlatch with performances by the dancing societies. The latter were elaborate dramas representing the abduction of certain individuals (with inherited rights to the performances) by supernatural beings who returned them, endowed with varied and often spectacular ceremonial prerogatives.

The Salish groups, who had fewer ceremonial prerogatives to announce and validate, gave potlatches to confirm the status of their chiefs. To demonstrate that he was worthy of the post, and thereby validate his status, the headman of a Salish lineage might stage such a performance years after he had nominally attained his position as leader of his extended family.

Too many years have passed since the last Chinook potlatch was given for us to have any detailed information on such variations as may have been made on the pattern along the lower Columbia. It seems most plausible to assume, however, that there was relatively little difference between their procedures and aims and those of their Salish neighbors.

The northernmost groups gave a minor variety that has been called a "face-saving" potlatch. When some misadventure befell a chief, or the heir to a chieftaincy—for example, if he stumbled and fell on some public occasion, or suffered any other public indignity—the damage to his honor could be repaired only by the formal distribution of gifts and the reaffirmation of his honorable status. The elaborateness of this performance depended to a large extent on the nature of the accident. If it was considered to have been a true accident and not the result of malicious human intent to demean him, a few small gifts sufficed to erase the damage to his dignity. If, however, there was any reason to believe that the affront had been deliberate, either through physical or magical means, a large and elaborate potlatch was called for. Among such groups as the Nootka and many of the Kwakiutl, where the function of the potlatch and its role in social integration was overtly recognized, a high-ranking guest at another chief's potlatch, when conducted to the wrong seat by the ushers, satisfied his honor by giving a single blanket to one of the hosts. In such a situation the host chief repaid this gift later on in the proceedings.

Competitive potlatches have received considerable attention in ethnographic literature because of their very spectacular nature. Two powerful rivals might give away and destroy thousands of dollars' worth of trade goods and money in the course of the contest. The destruction of property, of course, was to demonstrate that the chief was so powerful and so rich that the blankets or money he threw on the fire, or the "coppers" he broke, were of no moment at all to him. While such contests were held occasionally among many of the northern groups, they reached their highest development—or perhaps one should say their peak of bitterest rivalry—in two places: Fort Rupert and Port Simpson. It appears fairly clear that nearly identical factors led to this development in the two localities. It will be recalled that several neighboring Kwakiutl tribes moved into Fort Rupert when the Hudson's Bay Company post was established there, forming a loose confederation. Each of these tribes consisted of several local groups who, long ago, had formed fairly stable political entities, even though the local groups retained a certain independence of action as well as their individual property rights. Once the tribes occupied the common site, close to the trading post, they were faced with a very acute problem. It was inevitable that each tribe should sooner or later invite the others to potlatches. It is necessary to explain here that while the ranking of the individuals within each local group was well known, and in each tribe the lineages, and their respective chiefs, were graded in a well-established order of precedence from highest to lowest, there were no precise verbal designations for these sequences—that is to say, there were no native terms directly translatable as "first chief," "second chief," "third chief," etc. The crucial point, and the public recognition of a chief's claim to precedence, occurred at the time of the distribution of gifts to the guests. The highest-ranking chief was given the first gift—and ordinarily, to show respect for his rank, the largest single gift. The chief second in rank among the assembled guests was the recipient of the second gift, and so on in descending sequence. The chiefs of the newly organized Fort Rupert Confederacy had no precedents on which to base the relative rankings of the chiefs of the several tribes. This fact led them to initiate a series of potlatches in which certain of them asserted their claims to particular places—first, second, third, or fourth, and so on—in the consolidated precedence list. When two chiefs claimed the same place, the first one would give a potlatch, stating his claim; then the second would try to outdo him. Finally, one or the other gave away or destroyed more property than his opponent could possibly equal. The one who had been surpassed had no recourse. He could no longer contest his claim, for, in the native mind, it came to be regarded as ridiculous that an individual of few resources (and of course this involved not only the man, but his entire local group) should attempt to make a claim against someone who had demonstrated power and wealth.

The extremes to which these competitions were carried and the attitude that developed in Fort Rupert—that great expenditures were sufficient to validate any sort of a claim—are exemplified by the unique institution which those people created. This was the title of "Eagle." An Eagle was a person who had the special right to receive his gift before the highest-ranking chief was presented with his. At one time there were twelve Eagle titles at Fort Rupert. Investigation has revealed that most of these Eagles were not chiefs at all, but were men of intermediate or even common status who through industry and clever trading amassed great quantities of material wealth. Some of them, in addition, were backed by certain chiefs who recognized them as potential tools to assist in the downfall of some high-ranking rival. It is interesting to note that the Eagles made no pretenses at claiming tradition-hallowed names or crests, but assumed or tried to assume invented names that referred in some way to the privilege that they hoped to acquire—that of precedence in receiving gifts before the real nobles. There was even one individual who, in the early part of the last century, presumed to claim the right to receive his gift on the day *prior* to the potlatch. The chiefs would not tolerate this effrontery; when he insisted on his claim, they had him killed. Others of this *nouveau riche* contingent, however, managed to keep in the good graces of the chiefs and maintained their anomalous positions for many years.

After the nine Tsimshian tribes assembled at Port Simpson, they were faced with almost the identical problem regarding potlatch protocol. The order of precedence of the clan chiefs within each tribe had been established for a long time and was not subject to question. The intertribal rankings were not definite. Competitive potlatches, very similar to and quite as bitterly contested as those of the Fort Rupert Kwakiutl, became common. It is entirely possible that such contests occurred occasionally among various groups in the remote past when certain local groups assembled at common winter villages in the process of tribal amalgamation. These prehistoric competitions never were so frequent or involved such quantities of valuables as at Fort Rupert and Port Simpson. An interesting sidelight on these specialized potlatches is afforded by the fact that among the Haida at Masset, fictitious competitions were staged solely to add a little spice to the occasion. The putative rivals agreed, in private, to expend identical amounts so that the affair would come out a draw. Some Southern Kwakiutl chiefs are known to have done this also.

The economics of the potlatch are not particularly complex. A chief announced his plans to his lineage or extended family mates some time in advance. He would normally expect them to contribute wealth goods to the extent of their ability. The low-ranking members of the group gave furs, blankets, or money for a variety of reasons: to gratify their personal sense of participation in the group performance, to assure the esteem of their chief and fellow group members, or to ensure public recognition for themselves or their children at the time of the potlatch by being given names or being included in some ceremonial in at least a minor capacity.

This concept of participation on the basis of familial ties is most obvious among the northern groups, where, in theory, a potlatch was supposed to be given by a chief (and his lineage) to lineages of the opposite moiety. For instance, among the Haida, recent studies have made clear that certain types of potlatch given in honor of the children of a chief were actually given by the chief's wife and her lineage—the same lineage, of course, that the children belonged to—to the lineage of the husband and sometimes others of his moiety. Nonetheless, the husband and his close relatives contributed substantially to the accumulation of valuables to be distributed in honor of the children. Similarly, a Tlingit chief could count on his wife's brothers' contributing handsomely to his store of wealth intended for a potlatch given in the name of his lineage, even though the brothers-in-law were in the opposite moiety and would be among the guests at the affair. Such gifts were outright donations; no return was expected other than the sort of eventual turn-about-is-fair-play reciprocity we ourselves expect in connection with Christmas cards and dinner invitations. The presents the brothers-in-law received at the potlatch bore no relation to any such donations they might have made, but were scaled to each one's individual rank. The important compensation, in native eyes, was that at the potlatch the chief honored his own children and their lineage mates—members of the lineage of his wife's brothers—by formally presenting them, announcing their assumption of hereditary names and titles (of their own lineage), and arranging to have their ears pierced, or to have them tattooed. In other words, the potlatch was an occasion for the emphasis of unity of a group of relatives even where kinship was ostensibly broken by the unilateral structure of society.

The amount of property that the chief set as an objective depended on the size of the group or groups he intended to invite and the elaborateness of the spectacle he planned. Among the Kwakiutl divisions and the more northerly tribes, he might, if necessary, borrow blankets or funds to attain his goal. Such loans were usually for a set period of time—half a year or a year—and were ordinarily repayable by a sum larger than the initial loan. This loan, and its repayment, was a financial transaction entirely separate from and outside the potlatch and had no relation to potlatch payments or gifts. When the time came for the big event and the various genealogical claims had been announced and the prerogatives and crests displayed, the gifts were distributed. Among the northernmost tribes, where the potlatch guests had performed certain tasks such as the burial of the dead chief, the raising of a mortuary column, or the building or rebuilding of the chief's house, etc., the chiefs to whom these duties had been entrusted received special gifts said to be payments for the work done. The individual chiefs so honored were expected later on to reward their own relatives and retainers who had done the actual work. The same procedure held true among the Haida, for example, when certain chiefs were designated to tattoo crests on noble children of the host group. These chiefs were given "payments" for the tattooing, although they themselves had not func-

72. A Haida "copper" with engraved design. Some examples have painted designs. The ancient "coppers," hammered out of placer metal obtained in trade from the Copper River, do not ring when struck like those of European sheet copper, but emit a dull sound; the T-shaped ridge of the old specimens is not hollow, stamped out from the back, but is a solid mass of metal.

tioned as the artists. The actual tattooers were paid by the recipients of these payments. Eventually all these preliminaries were completed. The main potlatch gifts were presented in amounts that varied according to the rank of the recipient. (Of course the payments as well as the gifts were distributed in the order of rank.) On occasions when guests were invited from various distant localities, as, for example, when a Tsimshian chief invited Haida and Tlingit guests, a tactful host would present gifts to the principal chiefs simultaneously.

A special class of objects, called "coppers" in English, was intimately associated with the potlatch. These large shield-like sheets were hammered out of placer copper found somewhere along the

73. *A Southern Kwakiutl chief with one of his "coppers." Coppers like this with repoussé ornament were less common than those with shallowly engraved and/or painted designs, but were not necessarily more valuable. Courtesy of Smithsonian Institution.*

74. *A Southern Kwakiutl princess of the 1890s. She is holding a "copper," most of the top of which has been cut away in defiance of her father's potlatch rivals. Courtesy of Smithsonian Institution.*

reaches of the Copper River in Alaska (Figs. 72–74). Of course in historic times many were made of sheet copper obtained from white traders. These coppers were traded southward as far as Southern Kwakiutl territory. Among the Tlingit, Haida, and Tsimshian, it was almost essential that one or two of them be used at the potlatch in honor of the dead chief, on the assumption of his place by his successor, and that they be broken and thrown on the fire or into the sea. To these people the coppers were valuable, but they were not nearly so highly regarded as they came to be among the Southern Kwakiutl, among whom the value of a copper was augmented each time it was given away, whether in a potlatch or in connection with bride price or dowry. Some coppers are known to have attained values of several thousands of dollars.

The northwest Californians—provincials from the areal point of view—staged performances that, like the potlatch, revolved about the wealth and status concepts. In these, however, the family wealth in material treasures was merely displayed, and was not distributed amongst the spectators. Rights and prerogatives such as existed in the north were lacking, so these folk contented themselves with an exposition of their valuables, then thriftily stowed them away for another year.

MARRIAGE

Marriage was regarded as a social contract, not merely between the man and his wife, but between their respective families. The higher the rank of the couple, the greater the emphasis on this aspect; the concern of the individual's family revolved principally about the rule that a person should marry a spouse of corresponding social status. A chief, or heir to a chieftaincy, should marry the daughter of a chief, or at least the daughter of a man of high rank, closely related to a chief's line of descent. Throughout the area it was deemed essential for the groom's family to give a substantial quantity of valuables and goods—the "bride price"—to the girl's family. The higher the rank of the couple, the greater the amount of the bride price. In northwest California, where areal patterns were so often reduced to their bare essentials, a man's worth was gauged in terms of the amount of the bride price paid for his mother. Two aspects of the bride price should be noted. First, it was not, outside of northwest California, a quantity arrived at through close bargaining by representatives of the two social units; it was rather as large an amount as the groom's group were capable of giving, given the status of the couple. Second, the woman's family did not, through the so-called "sale," lose all interest and rights in her, but continued to be concerned about her welfare. Their continuing interest was usually expressed by a return gift or series of gifts made to the man's family. The Southern Kwakiutl carried this concept to its logical conclusion by a series of return gifts from a man to his son-in-law, or the son-in-law's group, to "buy back" his daughter. The completion of these payments did not signify that the couple were thereby separated, but it did permit her to remain with her husband without pressure of obligation. Since it was customary for the father-in-law to include various crests and ceremonial privileges in his gifts to his son-in-law, which of course were intended for the couple's children, acquisition of such prerogatives through marriage came to be an end in itself. Hence, during the period of population shrinkage, or perhaps even before that time, the Kwakiutl devised fictitious unions in which a young chief was "married to" an arm, or leg, or the house post, of another chief. The quantities of valuables given by both parties, which were of course distributed by each recipient in potlatches, redounded to the credit of both.

There were several varieties of preferred marriages. One of these, found among the northern nations who reckoned descent matrilineally, was cross-cousin marriage (that is, marriage to one's mother's brother's daughter, or to one's father's sister's daughter). A young chief who married his mother's brother's daughter was actually marrying the daughter of the man whose position, house, and properties he would eventually inherit, an obviously convenient and practical arrangement. Among the Kwakiutl groups, the Bella Coola, the Nootka, and their nearest Salish neighbors, a chief or a chief's son might seek to marry the daughter of some distant important personage to create useful alliances; or he might marry a woman of approximately equivalent rank from some extended family to which he was already related, or, if the actual blood kinship were not too close, from his own group. The advantages of marrying into a related family, or to a woman from one's own extended family, were, according to the Kwakiutl, Bella Coola, and Nootka viewpoint, that one thereby regained crests and privileges that had been given away in previous marriages, in the one instance, or, in the other, retained such valuable possessions within the group. The Bella Coola are said to have arranged intragroup marriages quite often for their chiefs and chiefs' heirs in order to retain the family prerogatives. In fact, some early investigators interpreted this practical measure as a strict rule of endogamy (a term meaning a prohibition against marrying outside of a certain defined group), such as is found with a rigid caste system. However, this was not a correct interpretation, for many Bella Coola not only married outside their extended family units, but outside their nation as well, acquiring spouses among the Bella Bella and Wikeno in some numbers. Proof of this practice may be found in the number of crests and ritual prerogatives among the Bella Coola that they state were obtained from one or another Heiltsuk division "in marriage," that is, as part of the gifts made by the bride's father to his son-in-law, and in the various rights of similar type found among the Heiltsuk that are reported to be of Bella Coola origin. The Coast Salish and Chinook—except for those living near and strongly influenced by Southern Kwakiutl and Nootka—having, as has been previously stated, a more rigid rule of patrilineal inheritance of their few prerogatives, did not transfer such rights to sons-in-law, and as they did not have a unilateral organization either, there was no particular advantage to their marrying relatives.

The Yurok and their immediate neighbors added a unique touch of their own to the areal patterns. Normally, a bride went to live in her husband's home. Occasionally, however, either to patch up an affair in which a man of few resources had become involved with a girl, or in a situation in which a man of importance had daughters but no sons and did not want to be without willing hands to serve him, a special arrangement was made, a "half marriage," as the Yurok translate their own name for the institution into English. In this type of marriage, slightly more than half the normal bride price was paid by the groom and his kin, and he went to live in his father-in-law's house, where, in effect, he worked out the balance of the bride price in services.

WARS AND FEUDS

The Nootkan and Kwakiutl tribes, and their neighbors to the north-ward, made war on occasion; those to the south carried on feuds. The distinction is much more than one of the scale of the military operation and number of people involved, although usually the feuds of the Salish, Chinook, and northwest Californians were carried on by a few individuals at a time. At times the northerners too had their feuds, in which the killing or injury of a kinsman was avenged by his relatives. But true warfare, aimed at driving out or exterminating another lineage or family in order to acquire its lands and goods, was a well-established practice in the north. In the discussion of recent histories of the various groups, some attention has been given to these northern wars of conquest. Some northern Tlingit lineage or lineages drove the Eskimo off Kayak Island; the Kaigani Haida forced some southern Tlingit to withdraw from part of Prince of Wales Island and established themselves there; the Tsimshian Kitkatla and Kitisu tribes, and apparently the Bella Bella as well, were doing their best to exterminate the Xaihais in order to take possession of their territory. Among the Nootka, bitter, long-drawn-out wars were carried on by various local groups and tribes for the express purpose of capturing the territory of their neighbors. In addition, the objective of frequent raids, some of them at quite long range, was to capture wealth goods and slaves. The Haida raids down into the Puget Sound area have been mentioned. Presumably the development of the concept of a war of conquest is to be attributed to the highly developed concepts of property right in lands and places of economic importance, and to a certain amount of actual population pressure in the north in aboriginal times.

The raid staged on the occasion of the death of an important person, whether or not he had died from natural causes, was a typically northern custom. The usually expressed purpose was that of "sending someone with the dead chief," or of "making other people mourn also." Such a party usually attacked and slew the first persons they met; sometimes even their own village mates were not exempted if the raiders encountered them offshore in a canoe.

After a successful attack the northern warriors beheaded their victims, brought the heads home, and usually set them up on tall poles in front of the village. Only the Tlingit scalped; they took the heads of fallen foe and removed the scalps on the way home.

Feuds were conducted in a different fashion among most of the Northwest Coast groups. After a slaying or an injury, the kin of the victim made an effort to retaliate, although sometimes the trouble could be smoothed over. In any case, whether or not revenge was taken, the customary method of settling the feud among almost all the groups, except the Kwakiutl and Nootka, was by payment of indemnities, or "weregild." When more than the initial offense had occurred, each injury to either side had to be paid for separately. Intermediaries were usually sent back and forth to negotiate agreements as to the proper amount of damages. It was at this time, in northwestern California, that the valuation put on a man according to the amount of bride price paid for his mother came into play. Elsewhere such neatly calibrated scales were not used; the aim was to demand enough compensation to embarrass and humble the opponents. Sometimes, among the Tlingit and probably their immediate neighbors, in cases where no blood-money settlement could be agreed upon, a chief or noble of the slayer's lineage would take it on himself to resolve the matter. He, of course, had to be of a rank as nearly as possible equivalent to that of the slain person. He donned the finest ceremonial regalia of his lineage. Then he went out of the house, dancing one of the slow, stately hereditary dances of his lineage as he approached the waiting foe. The courteous gesture on their part was to allow him the dignity of approaching to within a few yards of them before they evened matters by killing him.

FIVE

RELIGION

Native religious beliefs and practices on the Northwest Coast revolved about a series of patterns and concepts shared by all or nearly all of the groups participating in the areal culture. There was, of course, a good deal of variation in the detailed manifestations of these basic tenets, but from the broad point of view these differences are quite superficial. These fundamental principles that combined to give Northwest Coast religion its distinctive cast were: lack of systematization of beliefs on creation, cosmology, and deities; a rather vague notion of a remote, disinterested Supreme Being or Beings; a set of beliefs revolving about the immortality of certain economically important species of animals, combined with a series of ritual practices to ensure the return of those creatures; and, finally, the concept of the possibility of lifelong assistance by a personal guardian spirit. It is worth stressing that among these people, as among other American Indians, religious belief played an important part in everyday life. The preparatory rites and observances at the time of a fishing or hunting expedition, or an appeal to one's guardian spirit, were equally important parts of getting ready as the preparation of the fishing or hunting gear. The same principle applied to preparations for a potlatch or a war party.

The absence of systematized beliefs about the cosmos, and about

138

origins, and the failure to arrange the various deities and lesser supernatural beings in formal hierarchies, so characteristic of the religious
thought of many, though not all, of the simpler American Indian
cultures, strike us as somewhat inconsistent with a civilization like
that of the Northwest Coast, where so many patterns were refined
and enriched to an amazing degree. One may find, for example, that
among the members of a single tribe, or in neighboring tribes of the
same linguistic and cultural division, various individuals will give
completely different accounts of the ancient beliefs as to how the
world was supported, and whether the Land of the Dead was across
some distant river, somewhere in the sky, or in an underworld. Likewise, a god or spirit regarded by one informant as of great importance will be described as a minor personage by another. Strangely
enough, or so it appears at first, this anarchy of concept was most extreme among the more advanced groups from Vancouver Island
northward. It may well be that their influence on areal patterns also
affected their southern neighbors. The real reason for this apparent
disorganization of belief seems to have been that there was a very rich
unwritten literature of myths and legends current in the area; in fact,
several distinct cycles seem to have been represented, perhaps reflect-
ing the diverse origins of the several distinct linguistic divisions on
the coast. Each lineage or extended family took over some myth or
mythical episode, incorporating it into the official family tradition
to explain the origin of the kin group. Hence each of these social
units had its own official version of creation and the like. An early
investigator among the Bella Coola was told, for example, of a series
of superimposed heavens, in the highest of which the gods dwelt in
a single vast house. Just like the Indians who occupied a house in this
world, the gods were ranked in a series of statuses from the highest
to the lowest. As previously remarked, hierarchical structures of this
sort were not typical of the coastal culture. The Bella Coola were
therefore regarded as exceptional in the area for their systematization of religious thought. More recent studies, however, have revealed
that this concept was part of the origin tradition of a single Bella
Coola family line. Other Bella Coola were not familiar with the
details of the story, nor did they accept it as true at points where it
contradicted their own extended family traditions. Similarly, most
Haida conceived of the sky as a bowl-like firmament over the earth
and believed that on the upper side of the bowl was a Sky-World

inhabited by certain supernatural beings. However, one tradition, presumably the possession of some lineage and related to its legendary origin, describes a series of five Sky-Worlds, one over the other.

Beliefs in a Supreme Being were common to many of the Indian groups of our area. Typically, this deity was remote from the affairs of men and the world. He may formerly have taken a more active role. According to some myth cycles he was the Creator; in others, he was a Transformer (a being who went about in an existing but incomplete world, setting things in order). Nonetheless —and somewhat inconsistently—he was often addressed in prayer by the Indians. This was equally true of the Tlingit deity "Raven-at-the-head-of-the-Nass," the Haida "Power-of-the-Shining-Heavens," the Tsimshian "Laxha." The Nootka varied the pattern slightly by referring to and praying to the four "Great Chiefs," each of whom ruled a segment of the universe. In certain of their manifestations, Kwakiutl and Bella Coola Supreme Deities were closely associated with the sun. The Coast Salish (other than the Bella Coola) and Chinook seem to have been atypical, and apparently lacked any such concept. Farther south the data are less clear, because of the early shattering of the native culture, but the Athapascan-speaking tribelets on both sides of the California-Oregon border prayed regularly to a deity who had created their world.

A set of beliefs relating to the immortality of certain animal species was universal throughout the Northwest Coast. It seems fairly clear that in most cases the original concept, regardless of the group or groups of its origin, probably referred specifically to salmon. When one considers the spectacular phenomenon of the annual salmon runs, such a belief seems reasonable enough, especially to primitive people. At the same season every year, the same one of the five varieties of salmon would appear in great numbers in the bay or cove at the mouth of some stream, and after a short time would start upriver. A relatively small number, of course, were harpooned, netted, or trapped, but the majority proceeded to the spawning grounds far upstream, spawned, and died. Their lean, battered bodies lined the river banks and drifted back to the sea. It is doubtful whether the Indians understood the life cycle of these fish, or connected the spawning with the tiny new-hatched parr, or these with the adult salmon. Yet the following year the species appeared again. Hence, what could be more logical than the concept that the salmon ascended the streams to benefit mankind, died, and then returned to life? The general belief was that the salmon were a race of supernatural beings who dwelt in a great house under the sea. There they went about in human form, feasting and dancing like people. When the time came for the "run," the Salmon-people dressed in garments of salmon flesh, that is, assumed the form of fish to sacrifice themselves. Once dead, the spirit of each fish returned to the house beneath the sea; if the bones returned to the water, the being resumed his (human-like) form with no discomfort, and could repeat the trip next season. Since the Salmon-people's migration was considered to be voluntarily undertaken, it followed that it behooved human beings to take pains not to offend their benefactors. To return all the salmon bones to the water was one of the procedures believed to be essential. If some bones were thrown away on land, on resurrection the Salmon-person might lack an arm or a leg, or some other part, and he and his tribe would become angry and refuse to run again in the stream in which they had been so unappreciatively treated. All the Northwest Coast groups had long lists of regulations and prohibitions referring to the Salmon-people in order to continue to maintain good relations with these important beings.

This concept was extended to many other species. Herring and olachen, also seasonal species, were widely believed to have their own house under the sea (or to share the Salmon-people's house) and to behave the same way. The Nootka believed that whales, hair seal, and, on land, the wolves (not of economic, but of ritual importance) likewise had their houses, and emerged wearing their animal form like a replaceable garment. Even creatures who were not believed to live in "tribal" houses were considered immortal. Among the Yurok, and probably their neighbors as well, deer were thought to be resurrected in the same fashion, and it was believed that they deliberately entered the snares or exposed themselves to the fire of hunters who meticulously observed the rites that the Deer-people considered pleasing.

It was not only the beliefs themselves that unified a great part of the areal religious patterns, but also the rites and observances developed out of them. For example, a First Salmon ceremony was held over the first catch from each important stream or area, the purpose of which was to honor and to welcome the first of the species. Usually the fish was addressed as though it were a visiting chief of high rank; it was handled in a ceremonious way, and was frequently given offerings such as the sacred eagle down of the northern groups; it was cooked and eaten in a formal fashion. This type of rite, except for details of performance, was almost uniform everywhere, except at the very extremes of the area. Tlingit and Haida attached less importance to it, and performed it in more attenuated fashion than did their neighbors to the south. In northwestern California the ritual was integrated with a First Fruits rite (and, among the Karok, with a New Fire ceremony) and, as well, with the Wealth Display performances, into a cult-system that has been designated a World-Renewal cycle. Nevertheless, the First Salmon ceremony was performed in some form by all the groups of the coast, and even by a few of their peripheral and ruder neighbors of the interior.

By analogy, similar rituals were performed to honor other species, such as herring and olachen in the north, and smelt (or "surf fish") along the Oregon and northern California coasts. Other game, including sea and land mammals, was treated ceremoniously when killed, so that the spirit would be placated and would return to the hunter wearing a new body whose flesh and fur the hunter might take.

The significance of these rituals in honor of important animals led to the development of a priesthood, another distinctive trait of Northwest Coast culture. The procedure for handling the first of the season's salmon catch became so complicated, and the prayers addressed to the Salmon-spirits became so lengthy, that a specialist had to take charge. Rites of limited importance, like those of the bear hunter or mountain-goat hunter, became individual possessions and were transmitted from generation to generation as valuable secret techniques for securing game. Rituals for species that affected the general welfare, like salmon, likewise became private possessions, to be performed in the public interest. The Yurok ritualist had to be paid by public collection to recite his incredibly long formulaic prayers to the salmon and acorns; the Nootka or Kwakiutl chief ritually cleansed himself and performed his ceremony as part of his duty toward his people. It is particularly interesting that Nootka and a few Southern Kwakiutl ritualists made use of human bones and corpses in their rites, just like the Aleut whale-lancers, in the belief that the dead had great power over game.

It was generally accepted that an individual's control over his destiny—his good or bad fortune—depended on the intercession of a spiritual helper. The favor of such a being was won only after an arduous search, in which one cleansed one's self of taints offensive to supernatural beings by fasting, bathing in icy pools, scrubbing away the clinging aura of human sensuality with harsh flesh-mortifying bundles of twigs or nettles. Among the Tlingit, Haida, and perhaps the Tsimshian, there was a tendency toward a sort of inheritance of spirit helpers. That is, an individual went through the usual quest, but encountered a particular spirit or spirits that "belonged," as it were, to his maternal lineage. Simply performing these rites contributed to one's success, but in addition one might encounter a spirit who allowed himself to be subjugated if the quester were properly purified, and thenceforth served like Aladdin's djinni. Such a "guardian spirit" might confer power to cure the sick, to become a great warrior, to acquire wealth, or, among the tribes north of Puget Sound, might bestow the right to display some ceremonial performance representing the being himself. As a matter of fact, all the prized crests of the northerners were supposed to have been obtained originally through just this kind of supermundane authorization. The clan ancestor, among the northernmost groups, or the benefactor of the lineage among Kwakiutl and Nootka, appeared and conferred the right on all ensuing generations to use masks or symbols representing himself.

From the individual point of view, one of the maximum gifts a spirit could bestow was one that could be utilized to affect the fortunes of one's friends and neighbors. The best way to achieve that was to be granted the power to cure or cause illnesses. The "medicine-man," or "shaman" as he is called in the literature, was a power in the community. Many commoners who possessed no high social rank to bring them into the public eye found a compensatory prestige in shamanistic power. Everywhere the popular phrasing was that to be a shaman sent an individual on the road to wealth. Actually, the medicineman, although often well paid for curing the sick, could never accumulate enough valuables to offer serious competition to the chief, who, as lineage head, inherited not only economic rights and properties, but also the right to call on the produce of all the members of the family. What the shaman actually obtained was public recognition, either esteem or fear or a blend of both, far beyond that to which his modest birth would have entitled him. By performing the arduous cleansing rites and encountering a spirit who granted curing power one became a public figure, the cynosure of all eyes when the whole village congregated to watch the treatment of a patient. Illness was generally believed to be caused either by intrusion of small semi-animate objects that drove bullet-like into one's body, or by witchcraft, either of the contagious variety in which some enemy cast spells over bits of one's clothing, hair combings, etc., or of the type in which a wizard "sent" or "threw" disease-causing objects into one. From the Oregon coast northward the belief was held that one's soul might be lost, either stolen or just gone astray. Another possible cause of disease was a sort of contamination by a ghost or spirit, particularly if one were not ritually clean at the time of the encounter. The shaman's task consisted in summoning his spirit helper or helpers, usually by singing their songs and dancing, until the supernatural assistant bestowed the power to extract the disease object, find the strayed soul, or remove the contamination. Among some Salish groups, especially in the Puget Sound area, a dramatization of the journey in a spirit canoe in quest of the lost soul was a most spectacular performance.

The shamanistic regalia and gear varied. The Tlingit and Haida shaman allowed his hair to grow, and never combed it; the shaggy tangle was his badge of office. Among both these divisions he typically wore elaborately carved necklaces of bone, and had a special bone tube (Fig. 75) to blow sickness away and to catch souls. Haida medicinemen usually accompanied their songs with carved globular rattles (Fig. 71); some Tlingit and Tsimshian used "chief's rattles," carved with figures of the raven and the frog (Fig. 70); others used rattles of puffin beaks or deer hoofs (Fig. 69). The Tlingit shaman usually owned a variety of masks representing his familiars, and wore them as he danced when beginning a cure. Kwakiutl, Nootka, and Bella Coola donned turban-like headbands and neckrings of shredded and dyed red cedarbark as insignia of their professions. Some Salish shamans had peculiarly shaped boards painted with crude designs referring to their spirit helpers (Fig. 77); others carved representations of those beings (Figs. 78, 101).

The northwestern Californians varied the general shamanistic pattern of the area somewhat. Among these groups most shamans were women, in contrast to the north where the profession was predominantly, though not exclusively, a male one. The guardian spirit

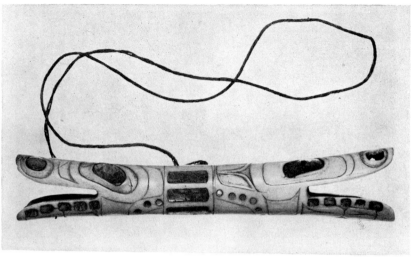

a

b

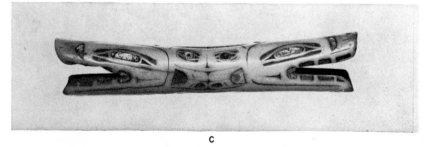

c

75. *Tsimshian (a, b), and Tlingit (c), shamans' "soul-catchers" carved of bone with abalone shell inlays.*

76. Carved shamans' amulets (a, b), and needlecase (c), of bone, from the Tlingit.

77. Typical spirit canoe boards, representing beings who assisted the shaman in his dramatized journey to recapture a lost soul. Probably from the Salishan Duwamish or some nearby group of Puget Sound. Northwest Coast artistic concepts have been replaced here by something quite different.

146

concept was played down. And although a Yurok, Karok, or Hupa
shaman had some sort of supernatural mentor, she acquired her power
principally through capturing, swal-
lowing, and learning to control the
semi-animate objects believed to
cause illness. She made considerable
use of a tobacco pipe and of smoking
in connection with her cures, and—
whispered gossips—in causing people to become ill so that she might
be paid for curing them.

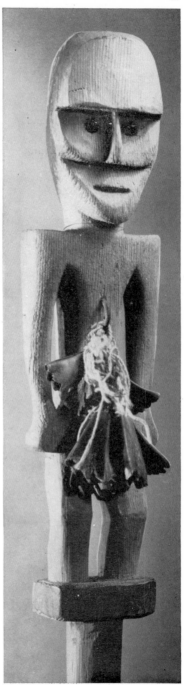

*78. A shaman's rattle from the Qui-
nault, a Salish tribe of western Washington. The rattle combines the form
of the shaman's guardian spirit with
the use of deer-hoof sounders. Artistically this specimen represents one distinctively Salish style.*

SIX

CEREMONIALS

O N THE Northwest Coast there were two principal centers of development of ceremonialism. One of these was among the Kwakiutl and Nootka, the other in northwestern California, where the Yurok, Karok, and Hupa interwove a series of rituals into the elaborate World-Renewal ceremonial cycle. The performances of the Wakashan-speaking groups were both unique and spectacular (Fig. 79). Essentially they were cycles of dramas revolving around a single theme: the protagonist's encounter with a spirit who kidnaps him, bestows supernatural powers upon him, then returns him to his village, repeating the experience of the ancestor from whom the performer inherited the right to the performance. If this sounds as threadbare and monotonous as a much-repeated plot, it should be pointed out that the Indian dramatists were able to elaborate as many variations and new twists with it as our playwrights do with our standardized boy-meets-girl theme. The Kwakiutl hero, depending on the particular version to which he was hereditarily entitled, might enact his kidnaping by slipping quietly away from the village, or he might pretend to be struck dead by the power of the spirit, then to be resurrected by public ritual. Or he might be pounced on by men wearing monstrous disguises who would carry him off bodily to the woods. After the proper period of hiding, during which he was sup-

148

79. Dramatis personae *of a Southern Kwakiutl Shamans' Society perform-ance, an old photograph. The crouching figures of the center front, with the masks representing wide bird-like beaks, represent the Bakbakwala-nūsīwa, the monstrous man-eating bird who possesses and inspires the Cannibal-dancer. The house posts on either side, in the background, repre-sent the Thunderbird, important in many Kwakiutl and Nootka family traditions; the central post is very unusual in style. At the left of the picture part of a painted board screen can be seen; this is the front of the cubicle in which the principal performer was kept.*

posed to be at the home of the spirit, he returned, or was escorted back, and had to be captured by his fellow villagers because he was so imbued with supernatural power that he was in a state of frenzy; and, finally, he demonstrated the powers with which the spirits had endowed him. These powers might consist of the right to display some sleight-of-hand tricks, or might involve the ability to trans-form himself into the spirit (or cause the spirit to appear). Some of the representations of spirits were in the form of stately dances by masked performers; others, portraying savage and war-like spirits ac-

80. A Southern Kwakiutl changeable mask. The outer mask represents a Wolf Spirit; by manipulating strings the dancer can open the hinged halves to reveal a representation of a supernatural bird-being.

cording to the fiction of the particular rites, had to be forcibly restrained from wreaking violent acts, or performed horrendous deeds and then were ritually calmed down by their attendants.

The skill of these Indians in elaborating sensational stage effects was unsurpassed among the natives of North America. Many of the masks have movable parts, or are arranged to change their form (Fig. 80); in the houses, tunnels and trap doors were prepared so that actors could "miraculously" appear and disappear; lines of hollow kelp stems concealed under the floor were used as speaking tubes, causing performers' voices to come from unexpected places, such as under the fireplace. Puppets and monsters flew across the house, over the "spirit room"; these were wooden figures strung from ropes (Fig. 81). It must be noted that these climactic displays occurred at night. In the huge houses lighted only by a blazing fire in the central hearth, such stage props as ropes from which figures were suspended and the strings that operated the movable parts of the masks were not easily seen.

In one of the dance cycles, the personage of highest rank was supposed to have been carried off, and on his return inspired by a Cannibal Spirit. According to the plot, the dancer periodically became frenzied (Fig. 82). To prevent him from killing and eating his fellows, he was fed specially prepared human corpses. It is highly improbable that corpses were actually used; as remarked previously, the Kwakiutl were past masters at producing realistic tricks for stage effects. The smoked carcass of a small black bear, for example, fitted with a carved head, would look convincingly like a well-dried human body at a little distance, and by firelight into the bargain. After his grisly meal the *Tanis* (or *Hamatsa* as the Southern Kwakiutl called him), that is, the personage inspired by the Cannibal Spirit, was ritu-

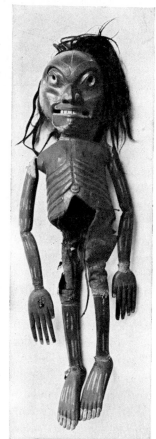

81. This jointed puppet represents the spirit presiding over the Kwakiutl Shamans' Society ceremonial (the dance series that includes the "Hamatsa," or Cannibal-dancer). Such puppets were displayed by chiefs giving the ceremonial and their principal guests. A simple sleight-of-hand trick made the objects appear to fly miraculously back and forth between host and guest, to symbolize the beginning of the performance. This specimen happens to be from the Haida, who used it with some of the performances they had acquired from the Kwakiutl. Courtesy of Smithsonian Institution.

82. *Dancer inspired by the Cannibal Spirit in a frenzied dance. Courtesy of University Museum, University of Pennsylvania.*

ally pacified by his attendants, and then he would dance quietly. After a while he might become excited again and, escaping from his attendants, might run among the audience where he seized certain persons by the arm and bit off large circular pieces of skin. This was not a trick, although it is said that usually the dancer actually cut off the piece of skin with a sharp knife concealed in his hand. The persons to whom this was done were not selected at random—it was arranged beforehand that they were to allow themselves to be bitten, and they were subsequently rewarded with special gifts. Finally, after a long period devoted to dances, temporary escapes, and ghoulish feasts, the dancer was sufficiently pacified so that he might safely be permitted to return to normal life.

Other spirits represented in the same cycle were War Spirits, Destroyers-of-Goods, Fire-throwers, and the like. Normally there was more than one dancer, or novice, since the younger relatives of the principal dancer were supposed to be abducted and inspired by less important spirits. As good dramatists, the Kwakiutl heightened the effect of the violent and frightening scenes by alternating them either with quiet, stately dances or with periods of clowning and horseplay during which any sort of practical joking was permissible, and at which no one might take offense.

The various dances have been compared to "secret societies" into which a person was initiated by public performance of the rite. Actually it was not the individual dance or performance that constituted the "society," but a series of them, ranked in order of importance in what the Indians refer to as a single "dance house." For example, among all the Northern Kwakiutl groups—the Wikeno, the Bella Bella, Xaihais, and Haisla—the Cannibal Dancer (*Tanis*) was the highest-ranking of a series that formed a single society or dance house, called by the Heiltsuk word for "shamans" (*tsitsiqa*). Among the Wikeno there were eight higher orders in the Shamans' Society:

83. Cannibal Spirit dancer. Courtesy of the University Museum, University of Pennsylvania.

1. The Cannibal Dancer
2. The Fire-throwing Dancer
3. The Grizzly Bear Dancer
4. The Rat Spirit Dancer
5. The Chewing Spirit, or Destroying Spirit Dancer
6. The Scalped Spirit Dancer
7. The Woods Spirit Dancer
8. The Ghost Dancer

Of lesser importance were a host of minor representations that may be performed by women and by men of low rank (the rights to use the individual performances were, of course, hereditary property).

Persons who were active participants in the Shamans' Society—and most of the higher orders had to be repeated annually for four years—were barred from attending the performances of the other principal society whose name in Heiltsuk means something like "The-Ones-Returned-from-Heaven" (*Dluwulaxa;* sometimes the word *"Mitla,"* which also seems to refer to descending from above, is used). The highest-ranking dances of this society are as highly esteemed as those of the Shamans. The principal differences between the two societies lie in that performances are held at different times of the year (the Shamans usually perform in the fall, The-Ones-Returned-from-Heaven in the spring); the novices in the latter series are supposed to be taken up into the sky; and there is usually only a single order among The-Ones-Returned-from-Heaven who performs violent acts.

Another society among these groups, the Nutlam (*Nułam*), was again separate and distinct. The name is apparently not translatable; it may be an archaic word, long gone out of ordinary use. The origin traditions of the ceremony relate that originally Wolf Spirits abducted ancestors of certain extended families, who, on their return, behaved like wolves, killing and eating dogs when frenzied. This was the characteristic act of the Nutlam novices. There does not seem to have been a ranked series of orders in this society. It seems likely that this may have been the most ancient of all these performances, for the now meaningless term "Nutlam," which is associated with Wolf Spirits in one way or another—usually with the act of dog eating, and, of course, with an initiatory performance into an exclusive society—is found as an obvious borrowing among many neighbors of the Northern Kwakiutl.

Most of the Southern Kwakiutl groups had a single secret society that includes a hodgepodge of all the performances of the Shamans' Society, The-Ones-Returned-from-Heaven, and the Nutlam. At least one division, however—the Koskimo and neighboring tribes of Quatsino Sound—had a separate ceremony called the "Nutlam," in which the initiates were supposed to be carried off by Wolf Spirits who gave them various dances and display privileges to use on their return. This was the same as the major ceremony of the neighboring Nootka, except that the Nootka called their ritual by the word for "The Shamans," and relegated the term "Nutlam" to a minor performance during the ceremonial. Dog eating was not practiced by either the Koskimo tribes or the Nootka in recent times, but may have been at one time, since a few Salish and Quileute groups of northwest Washington state, in their obvious borrowings of the Nootka version of the ceremonial, included the macabre act in their rituals.

Northward, the various Tsimshian tribes possessed both The-Ones-Returned-from-Heaven Society and the Nutlam. Many of the individual dances or orders of the former were known by their Heiltsuk names, indicating the source of the complex. A few Coast Tsimshian chiefs, through either marriage dowries or capture of the masks and other ceremonial regalia in war—a legitimate mode of acquisition—had acquired the right to perform various dances of the Shamans' Society, for which, once again, they used the Heiltsuk names. (They must, of course, have captured prisoners who were made to teach them the rituals.) Tlingit and Haida seem to have been in the process of acquiring the performances during the historic period, and were just beginning to integrate them into the system of lineage crest-display dances.

Aside from a few Gulf of Georgia Salish who had obtained Southern Kwakiutl masks and dances, and the Olympic Peninsula groups who imitated the Nootka Shamans' Dance, the prevailing Salish ceremonial pattern consisted of semi-competitive "guardian-spirit singings," in which various individuals, not only shamans but men with hunting or war power, sang the songs taught them by their tutelary spirits, while friends and neighbors formed a chorus. The lack of variety in these performances was apparently compensated by the enthusiasm with which they were carried on. The same guardian-spirit singing was known on the lower Columbia, and along a good part of the Oregon coast.

84. Hupa White Deerskin dance. The two dancers in the foreground are displaying large obsidian blades, an important type of treasure on the lower Klamath River. Courtesy of A. L. Kroeber.

The Yurok, and their Karok and Hupa neighbors also, performed a cycle of rituals in spring and fall with the avowed purpose of "renewing the world," ensuring an abundance of wild crops and salmon, and preventing disasters like floods and famine. A great part of this procedure was carried out by a priest at each place—for the rites were inseparably linked with certain localities to which the performance was restricted. The priest, with one or more assistants, performed a series of ritual acts, proceeding from one sacred spot to another, reciting a tremendously long formula that was actually a narrative relating how the ceremony had been established by an ancient race of supernatural beings. At or near the end of this long recitative, dances that were more or less frankly entertainment and for display of the wealth and treasures of important men were held. Normally there was a competitive element about the dances. Groups of men performed in turn, each group representing one of the nearby villages, and each group was equipped with valuables by the rich man of that place. There was a definite attempt to develop a climactic effect: at first the dances were brief, with few performers and valuables of small moment. As the days passed, more dancers participated; the performances themselves were longer; and each rich man brought out more and better treasures for his dancers' use. On the final day the greatest treasures—the crown jewels, so to speak—were displayed. There were two types of these dances, called in English the "White Deerskin" and the "Jumping" dances. Each had its own special regalia and valuables. In the former, the dancers carried skins of albino or oddly colored deer, the heads stuffed and adorned with bright-red woodpecker scalps (Fig. 84). Two, or sometimes four, men carried the highly prized large obsidian blades instead of skins, and danced back and forth in front of the line. In the Jumping Dance the performers marched in a line, and at certain places in each song gave a series of leaps, from the village to one of the sacred spots that had been renewed and cleansed by the priest. The principal ornaments consisted of wide buckskin bands, tied across the forehead with the ends flapping loose, each decorated with a sort of feather mosaic made out of fifty bright-red scalps of the pileated woodpecker, bordered by other feathers and white fur. At the end of the ceremony, each rich man retrieved his treasures from the dancers and took them home.

SEVEN
_____

THE CYCLE OF LIFE

The Northwest Coast people, like all others—ourselves included—considered that there were certain critical periods in the life of the individual, points of transition from one status to another, that required special care and attention. In their view, his behavior at that time determined the course of his subsequent life. There was also the feeling that the individual, at certain of these periods, might be dangerous to others. Therefore various procedures were carried out to ensure the well-being of the individual and his relatives and friends as well.

The occasions regarded as particularly significant by all these tribes were: birth, a girl's puberty, and death. There were, of course, numerous minor rites practiced by the several groups under consideration, such as specified ways of disposing of the first baby tooth —or all of the baby teeth—that a child shed, some kind of formalities connected with the first game a boy killed, or the first basketful of roots or berries a girl collected unaided, and so on. Marriage was an occasion for formalities and festivity, particularly if the couple were of high rank, but it was not considered to have the crisis aspect of the other life stages.

It would be out of place in a summary of this kind to relate in detail the multitude of observances of all the groups of the area.

158

A few generalized statements must suffice. Procedures for ensuring the individual's well-being were most emphasized at birth, of course. Commonly, there were privately owned magical techniques to ensure long life, success in some particular career such as canoe making, gambling, and the like, as well as rites that were common knowledge, such as methods of disposing of the end of the umbilical cord when it had been detached. The infant's mother was usually secluded for a varying number of days, during which she was kept on a restricted diet, being permitted no (or few) fresh foods, and being universally enjoined against eating fresh salmon. At the end of the set period she was ceremoniously restored to normal life, usually by a ritual bathing. Among some of the groups, the father's diet and activities were somewhat restricted during his wife's lying-in. Most of the northern nations, believing that twins were mysteriously related to the Salmon Spirits, required parents of twins to camp far from salmon streams and to subsist on a diet of dried foods for a long time, lest the Salmon Spirits be offended. Among these groups a twin, when grown, was believed to have special power to cause bountiful runs of salmon.

At the onset of a girl's puberty she was invariably secluded. Her presence was believed to be offensive to the spirits of Salmon and other game; therefore she was prohibited from approaching the river and from eating fresh fish or meat. The northwestern Californian pubescent was restricted to a diet of very thin acorn mush. All the groups believed that by doing certain types of work, performing certain magical procedures, and, of course, by faithful obedience to the taboos, the girl would become an industrious woman, would bear many healthy children, and would live long. By remaining in seclusion at the proper times, by observing all the rules and so avoiding the offending of salmon and other important fish and game, she protected the food supply of her family and did not, by her contaminating presence, endanger the luck of any fisherman or hunter. Bathing rituals normally occurred during the period of seclusion or at its termination.

When a person died his kin were torn between grief at the loss and fear of the ghost. Among the southern divisions, the body was removed from the house as soon after death as possible. Wakes, at which family dirges were sung, were held by the northern groups, as far south as the Gulf of Georgia. When a chief died, a wake might last several nights. Removal of the body through a hole in the wall was almost universally practiced, so that the living would not have to follow the path of the dead as they passed in and out through the door. The method of disposal of the body varied. The Tlingit, Tsimshian, and Haisla cremated their dead. The body of a shaman, however, was put in a little grave-house on a point overlooking the sea. The body of a Haida was also placed in a grave-house. A mortuary pole would eventually be carved and set up for a Haida chief, and his remains transferred to a niche in the back of the pole, or to a box placed on top. A Haida who died far from home was cremated, however, and only the charred bones and ashes were brought home. Bella Coola traditions indicate that long ago their forefathers used to practice cremation. In more recent times they, like their Heiltsuk, Southern Kwakiutl, and Nootka neighbors, wrapped the dead in cedarbark mats, then placed them in wooden boxes, which they lashed high in the branches of a tree, or stowed away in a cave, or, more recently, buried in the ground. Some of the Gulf of Georgia Salish followed the same custom; others, that of their kin of Puget Sound and western Washington, and of the Chinook groups, who placed the body in a canoe, usually raised off the ground on a sort of scaffolding. The northwest Californians interred their dead. Everywhere the personal possessions of the deceased were buried with him, burned, or deposited at the grave. In the north a potlatch was held during which most of the wealth of a dead chief and his family was given away to the members of the "opposite" moiety or clan who had done the burying, carved and erected the mortuary or memorial column, and rebuilt the house of the chief's successor. The mortuary potlatch given in honor of a chief was indubitably the most important affair of this type among Tlingit, Haida, and Tsimshian.

Almost everywhere along the coast, both male and female mourners (the immediate family, had the deceased been a man of little consequence; the entire group, had he been a chief) cut their hair short in sign of mourning. Among some groups women also scratched their faces to indicate mourning. Usually both the principal mourners and the pallbearers had to be ceremonially bathed or otherwise purified to remove the contaminating influence of the dead, or actually of the ghost, before they could resume their normal lives.

EIGHT

ART

A̲ʀᴛ, ᴘᴀʀᴛɪᴄᴜʟᴀʀʟʏ carving in relief or in the round, was highly developed on the Northwest Coast. This applies to the region from the lower Columbia northward; the northwestern Californians and their neighbors did not participate in this artistic tradition, although they did decorate some of their small utensils with neat, if simple, geometric patterns. It was among the more northerly nations that the famous sculptural art, one of the finest in aboriginal America, came into full bloom.

There were two major stylistic divisions of this art, as well as several minor derived ones. The two principal strains, which were probably originally related, differed primarily in that one stressed applied design and formalization of representation, while the other was more fully sculptural and three-dimensional, combining realism with an impressionistic suppression of non-essential detail. In the north, the Haida, Tsimshian (including all the Tsimshian subdivisions: Coast, Gitksan, and Niska), and, to a slightly lesser degree, the Tlingit, developed a highly standardized style in which conventionalized forms were used to decorate innumerable objects. Symmetry and rhythmic repetition were accentuated. The Wakashan-speaking groups just to the south developed a simpler but more truly sculptural and vigorous style, which stressed mass and movement rather than conventionalization (it must be noted that the northern carvers, when they wished, could produce restrained, highly realistic works of great merit, as, for example, portrait masks and helmets [Fig. 85]). In relatively late historic times, the north-kan artists, began to incorporate some of its conceptual principles into their work. They managed to retain, however, the vigor of their old style, and the old sculptural quality, so that their carvings can always be distinguished.

The Coast Salish imitated the older Kwakiutl and Nootka carving. Much of their work was a simplification of an already boldly simplified style, so that it seems crude in comparison with its prototype. There were several minor local patterns among the Salish and Chinook that appear to reflect minor differences in sources of inspiration —that is, whether the group in question had closer cultural contacts with the Southern Kwakiutl or with the Nootka, and also, the distance from these sources. As far south as the Columbia River, traces of Wakashan stylistic influence may be seen, although the original three-dimensional treatment was crudely reduced to two dimensions, and a few purely local touches were added, perhaps because of influences from the interior.

The origins of the styles are unknown. Most authorities, however, agree that their perfection and standardization indicate a lengthy developmental history. The first European explorers in the area, Cook and Dixon, saw and collected objects at Nootka Sound and on the Queen Charlotte Islands stylistically identical with those made a century and more later. There is no evidence of any important modification of stylistic patterns during the historic period other than their gradual deterioration through disuse toward the end of the last century and the early decades of the present one. This decline resulted from loss of interest due to the rapidly accelerated acculturation of the Indians and to their nearly complete missionization, which was accompanied by pressure brought to bear by missionaries in favor of the abandonment of all pagan customs. The impairment of the art style was also affected to some extent by the legal prohibition of certain customs, like the potlatch, with which much of the art was associated. At the present time this great art is virtually extinct.

Such earlier developments as can be reasonably well documented during the nineteenth century point to its strength and vigor prior

85. Haida portrait masks. These specimens were made to represent real persons, probably in connection with a performance involving representation of the killing and miraculous resuscitation of the person concerned. The Kwakiutl excelled in the making of such portrait masks.

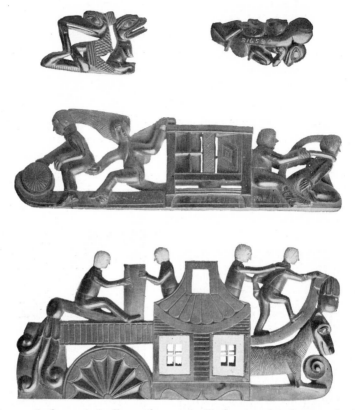

86. *Some of the artistically rather poor "tobacco pipes" carved of slate by the Haida, and collected by the United States Exploring Expedition from Hudson's Bay Company personnel on the Lower Columbia in 1841. Courtesy of Smithsonian Institution.*

to the historical deteriorations just mentioned. For example, some time quite early in the nineteenth century, or perhaps in the closing years of the eighteenth, the Haida began to mine a soft black slate that occurs in one locality in the Queen Charlottes, and to carve it into pipes and pipestems for sale to whites. A number of reasons lead us to believe that this work began under white stimulus. First, the earliest explorers and fur traders who visited the Haida do not mention any articles of slate. Second, pipes were not known to the Haida or their neighbors of the north until smoking was introduced by whites. Finally, the pipes seem to have been made purely for sale or barter, not for native use. By the time the United States Ex-

ploring Expedition, under Lieutenant Wilkes, U.S.N., visited the
Oregon Territory in 1841, where they were given quantities of specimens from the Queen Charlotte Islands by the Hudson's Bay Company personnel at Fort Vancouver (Fig. 86), the Haida were turn-
ing out considerable numbers of elaborate and ornate—and most
certainly unsmokable—slate pipes, most of them obviously poor imitations of white seafarers' scrimshaw work. Some of these objects
show considerable technical skill, but artistically are pretty sad.
During the next two or three decades, however, the aboriginal art
style, latent in the consciousness of the carvers, began to come to
the fore, submerging the clumsy copying of alien patterns. Some of
the "pipes" were still made, but came to be decorated with native
motifs (even during the "scrimshaw" period, carvers occasionally

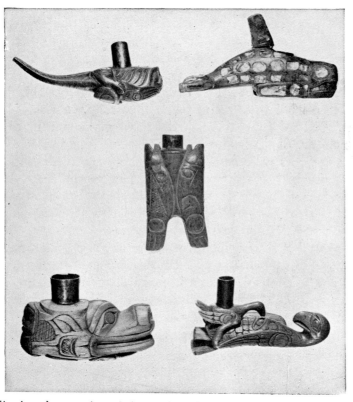

87. *Tlingit tobacco pipes (of wood with metal bowls), of the late nineteenth century, made after popularization of the custom of smoking among
that people.*

utilized aboriginal themes, though in a stiff awkward manner [Fig. 87]). The Haida artists began to carve models of "totem poles," decorated boxes, and feast dishes, in slate, and by the 1880s the ancient style dominated the slate carving to the point where the specimens of purely classic type and of considerable artistic merit were being produced (Fig. 88). In other words, the basic tenets of the style were strong enough to dominate the introduced complex, in which a new material was first used to copy new forms (pipes and scrimshaw work) for a new purpose (for sale as curios), suggesting that the native art was firmly rooted in, and thoroughly harmonious with, the native culture.

This whole art, both among the three northernmost nations and the Kwakiutl and Nootka (and the Bella Coola), was aimed at the depiction of the supernatural beings, in animal, monster, or human form, who according to lineage or clan traditions had appeared to some ancestor, or, in some instances, had transformed itself to human form and become an ancestor. In either case the descendants of that ancestor, in the proper line, inherited the right to display symbols of the supernatural being to demonstrate their noble descent. Whether painted or carved, the motifs are often referred to as "crests," and were much like the heraldic emblazonments of European nobility. Similarly the masks and other appurtenances of the dancing societies were hereditary lineage property (although they, and the rituals they represented, could be formally bestowed outside the family line under certain conditions, or captured in war). Thus the art style itself, through the objects made according to its dictates, was intimately linked with the social organization, rank, and status, as well as the ceremonial patterns, of the northern groups.

Perusal of the illustrations in this volume showing Tlingit, Haida, and Tsimshian objects will make the special features of the northern art style clear, and will demonstrate its aesthetic value. For orientation, its major characteristics are listed below.

1. Whether two-dimensional (painting or low, flat relief) or three-dimensional (carving in high relief or full round), it was essentially an *applied* art. Thus its forms were typically adapted primarily to the shape of the object decorated. This was true even of the figures carved in high relief, like those on "totem poles" and spoon handles of mountain-goat horn, in which they appear to be contained within the mass of the material. Masks, because of their spe-

88. *Slate carving comes of age. Traditional figures, model totem poles, and carved boxes, made by Haida artists in the latter half of the nineteenth century. The second figure from the upper left is a representation of the famous "Bear-mother" tale, a part of the origin tradition of certain important clans.*

cialized function, formed the only important exception to this rule.

2. Conventionalization of form was carried to an extreme degree. However, this did not take place in a random manner, in one way in one specimen and differently in another, but according to certain principles. The first of these resulted from adaptation to the object decorated, as just mentioned. The second was based on what amounted to a passion for symmetry and balanced design. This may be observed most clearly in two-dimensional design, where, for balance, the figure was treated as though it had been split lengthwise and spread out flat, as it were, on the level surfaces, or wrapped around the sides of the whole object (Fig. 89). There were many ways of accomplishing this. One was by "splitting" the figure into two separate halves, each half then being shown in profile, head to head, tail to tail, or back to back. Another slightly more complex mode of representation was to "split" the subject from the neck back, showing the head and face in front view, with the two halves of the body spread out on either side. Third, the artists emphasized certain areas in which they were interested, such as the head and face, and sometimes the paws or tail, and minimized or suppressed other parts. This trend was related to the fourth factor in conventionalization: the exaggeration and standardization of certain details for identification of the being represented. As already remarked, the objective of the art was to depict definite symbols, the property of the clans and lineages. To render these symbols recognizable, certain distinctive features were selected, and consistently used. The following list enumerates a few of these typical keys to identification:

Bear: Short snout, large teeth, protruding tongue, large paws and claws
Wolf: Long snout, large teeth
Beaver: Prominent incisors, holding stick in forepaws (forepaws sometimes raised to this position without stick), wide, flat, scaly (cross-hatched) tail
Killer whale: Large mouth with prominent teeth, long "dorsal fin," whale flukes
Raven: Wings (usually), long straight beak
Eagle: Wings (usually), heavy down-curved beak
Sculpin: Two short dorsal fins, spines around mouth

It should be added that occasionally, when realism was required, the artists discarded their conventionalizations and produced portrait masks and helmets of amazing fidelity.

89. Northern designs, showing methods of two-dimensional applications of three-dimensional design concepts. Note various ways in which the figures are portrayed as though they had been split and spread out. All these happen to be Haida, but Tlingit and Tsimshian artists used this technique. a, Beaver design from basketry hat; b, sea-monster painting on a screen; c, painting representing a bear; d, carving (seen from above) on wooden hat representing a sculpin; e, tattoo design representing a being called "wasgo," which combined characteristics of the whale and the wolf.

3. There was a strong tendency to fill all vacant areas, showing a sort of horror of blank spaces. For this reason, for one thing, when a series of figures are carved, as on a "totem pole" or a spoon handle, they are interlocked, with no intervening spaces. The "eye element," a rectangle with rounded corners, containing a lenticular form surrounding a circular one (the iris of the eye), was often used simultaneously as filler and to indicate arm and leg joints. Another common technique for avoiding blank space, especially in two-dimensional design, consisted in filling in the body area of the figure with a sort of schematic anatomical view. Occasionally this had a purpose, as in cases in which the being had eaten someone or something in the legendary episode in which he appeared. Even where such "X-ray" views or anatomical sections had no bearing on the myth, however, the device was frequently used.

4. Movement in the artistic sense—that assists in carrying the viewer's eye from one part of the composition to another—was achieved in several ways. The interlocking of a series of figures, mentioned above, contributed to that effect, particularly when the large principal figures were alternated with smaller ones in a rhythmic sequence. This device was used frequently, though not exclusively, by Tsimshian totem-pole carvers. Painted lines typically vary in width, being thicker at the centers and tapering toward the ends. (In self-enclosing elements, like the "eye" design unit, the upper and lower margins usually taper toward the sides.) Movement as well as accentuation was frequently given to carvings by flowing painted lines.

Two-dimensional design—either painting in red and black, other than that used for accent and embellishment of high relief carving, or incised or very low relief carving—was applied to a great variety of objects: storage boxes, "settees" or chiefs' backrests, cradles, globular wooden rattles, canoe hulls and paddle blades, house fronts, the highly valued shield-like "coppers," "oil cups" of wood or mountain-sheep horn, shamans' charms and "soul catchers" of bone, horn, or ivory, and as well to buckskin, elkskin, or caribou-skin robes. In the field of textiles twined-woven spruce-root hats were painted with crest decorations, and a few plain woven Chilkat blankets have been collected that have designs painted on them. It is not known whether this was an older practice than weaving designs in panels; it may have been, and persisted into historic times.

An early historic reference to robes "with designs in blue, yellow, black, and white" can refer only to the usual type of Chilkat blankets that we know from historic times. Incidentally, the typical Chilkat blanket and "dance shirts" with patterns woven in, and the older dance aprons and leggings, are the only objects we know that were regularly made by women in the classic northern art style. It is not that there was a specific taboo involved, but the motifs did not ordinarily lend themselves to the geometricity of basketry decoration. Hence, women did not learn the working principles of the art as did the men interested in painting and carving. (It should be noted that only certain men—not all—learned the principles of the art style and applied them to painting and carving.) There are a very few—and they are few indeed—Tlingit and Haida baskets that bear woven crest designs rather than the usual geometric patterns. As a matter of fact, in the manufacture of Chilkat blankets, male artists made pattern boards that the women weavers, technicians but not artists, carefully and methodically followed. The only other woven representative designs made by women in the area were the whaling scenes, schematic but with a certain verve, imbricated on the spruce-root hats of the Nootka. These, like the male-made Nootkan art products, vary from the northern pattern in their angularity, detail-less motifs, and extensive open areas.

Carving was done in high relief or the full round, in the classic tradition, in diverse materials and applied to a variety of objects. Most authorities are agreed, however, that this type of work was originally developed around a complex of woodworking, and then secondarily extended to horn, bone, ivory (traded from some Eskimo source), and even an occasional piece of stone. The handles of mountain-goat horn spoons, many feast dishes in their entirety, sealing and halibut clubs, figures mounted on canoe prows, "totem poles," the shanks of halibut hooks, speakers' staffs, and a host of other artifacts, were executed in high relief.

The Wakashan version of this art, as was remarked before, differed in a number of ways from that of the northernmost nations. Basically, it was more frankly sculptural, and less an applied art. Whereas even in full-round carving the work of the northerners gives the impression of being contained within the original volume of the log, horn, or bone on which the carving was done, Kwakiutl and Nootka artists did away with the confines of their material,

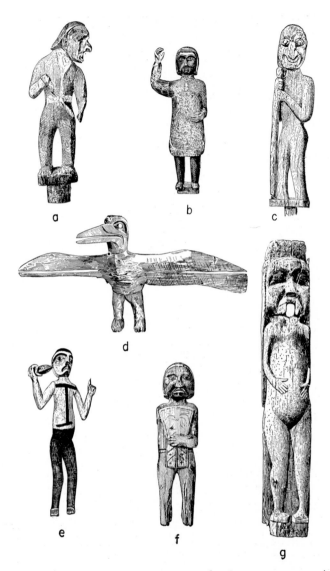

90. *Old Southern Kwakiutl sculpture: a, b, figures representing Chief Speaker, used in potlatch; c, figure representing caricature of Speaker; d, a grave monument; e, represents a chief's attendant killing slaves and breaking coppers; f, represents a counter of blankets holding a copper; g, part of a house beam used as a grease trough.*

91. Old-style Nootkan house post. From W. A. Newcombe Collection.

92. Memorial to a famous recent Nootka chief, erected at Friendly Cove, on Nootka Sound, about 1900. The pyramidal framework was originally covered with canvas, and represented the snow-capped peak on which the Thunderbird traditionally dwelt.

cutting it away into new planes, and expanding beyond it by adding appendages—for example, the outstretched wings of a Thunderbird, or the prominent "dorsal fin" of the killer whale (occasionally northern artists added pieces to carvings, especially long beaks of certain birds carved on "totem poles," but this was not characteristic of their work). The Wakashan carving was less often applied to objects of utilitarian use, and hence was freer of the restraints of an applied art. The themes depicted were much less rigidly conventionalized; instead, there was a stress on realism of significant areas. At the same time large open areas were tolerated, and minor details were suppressed, so that the sweeping lines lead directly to the key areas and the eye is not distracted by secondary space-filling motifs. All these features of the Wakashan style combine to give great strength and force. Its impressionistic simplicity gives it a certain "primitive"

93. A Southern Kwakiutl mask representing the Thunderbird.

94. Two Nootkan masks, representing spirits of a minor ceremonial.

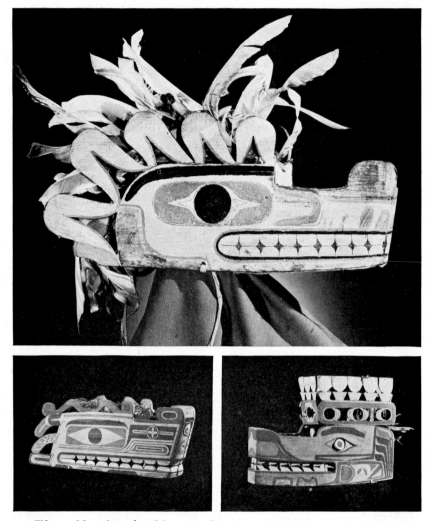

95. *Three Nootkan headdress-masks, representing supernatural wolves and the serpent-like spirit of lightning.*

cast, but also boldness and vigor (Figs. 90–96). It is interesting to note that where Tlingit art differed from that of the neighboring Haida and Tsimshian, it was in the same direction, toward a simplified realism. Some Tlingit work is very similar to Wakashan art in treatment and forcefulness (Fig. 99). It may be that such carving is closer to the original style from which Haida and Tsimshian (and some Tlingit) art was evolved.

96. *Recent Southern Kwakiutl carving, showing fusion of Wakashan style and Northern influences. The upper figure is the Thunderbird, an important crest among Kwakiutl and Nootkan ranking families; the lower figure is the Tsonokwa, a legendary ogress. The carving, a memorial post in a cemetery, is about 17 feet tall.*

97. *(Below) Recent Nootkan house posts, showing adaptation of Northern influences in carving. Artistically, in their coherence and subtle restraint, these carvings are superior to Northern work. Photographs by C. F. Newcombe, at Clayoquot, British Columbia, 1903; W. A. Newcombe Collection.*

Archaeological materials, chiefly from the lower Fraser, reveal an old art style that contrasts markedly with the classic northern pattern. Yet these ancient objects fit the artistic traditions which the historic Coast Salish derived from their Kwakiutl and Nootka neighbors (Figs. 100–102). This archaeological material thus fits the hypothesis just suggested: that the Wakashan style, and its Salish derivatives, may have been the old form. Gradually the ancestors of the historic Tlingit, Haida, and Tsimshian modified that basic pattern into the subtle, more symmetrical, and also more static and more rigidly standardized style that was in use at the time of early historic contacts and was continued with no essential change till the closing decades of the nineteenth century.

"Totem poles." No discussion of classic Northwest Coast art can be complete without a mention of the famous "totem poles." The term is quoted because it is something of a misnomer. Strictly speaking, a totem among primitive peoples the world over is a creature or object associated with one's ancestral traditions, *toward which one is taught to feel respect and reverence*—true totemism involves a basic attitude of religious awe. The Australian aborigines, like many other totemic peoples, do not kill their totem animals for food, even in times of hardship. Other groups have rituals to propitiate their

98. Two Bella Coola masks. These people had a number of masks of this type, with a sort of corolla around the central face. In addition they used numerous masks of Kwakiutl type, which they had acquired from their Kwakiutl neighbors.

99. Tlingit shamanistic figurines, which perhaps represented intended victims of black magic. This type of simplified but vigorous art is probably a holdover of a very old Northwest Coast art style, preserved by Nootka and Kwakiutl and imitated in a crude way by the Coast Salish.

totemic species. Not so the Northwest Coast Indians. There a person with an Eagle, Raven, Bear, or other crest had no particular regard for creatures of that species. It was not the biologic species in general that was of importance in his clan or lineage tradition, but a single specific supernatural being who had used the form of an eagle, raven, or bear. The Indian had no compunctions whatsoever about killing

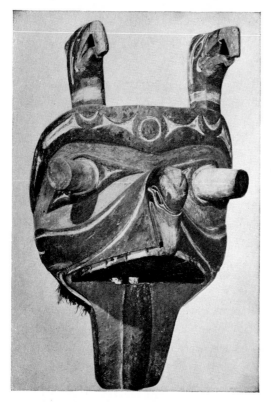

100. Coast Salish "sxwaihwai" mask. This mask represents one of a special group of supernatural beings connected with bird-spirits (note the form of ears and nose) developed on the Lower Fraser River and elaborated in the Straits of Georgia region.

contemporary representatives of these species. In discussing pride in one's ancestry, we have already drawn the comparison between the crests and European heraldic quarterings. From the point of view of use, the crests can be compared to a cattle brand that the modern Western cowman burns not only on his animals to establish legal ownership, but on the gatepost of the corral, on the wings of his chaps, on the doorjamb of his house, and all sorts of places, because it is his brand and he likes it. Similarly, the northern nations along the coast took pride in their crests and sought to display them as often and in as many ways as possible.

Several varieties of totem poles (we may dispense with the quotes now and use the popular term) with varying functions were set up. The first was the memorial pole, erected by a deceased chief's heir as part of the process of assuming his predecessor's title and prerogatives. Such poles were erected along the beach in front of the village. Among the Southern Tlingit and the various Tsimshian divisions this was the principal kind in use in historic times. Another

type, the mortuary pole, was set up alongside the grave of the deceased chief. Sometimes it actually constituted the grave, since the
box containing the remains might be placed in a niche in the back
of the pole, or was supported on top of it. The house-portal poles
were a third type. They were built onto the front of the house and
rose high above it, with a large opening, forming the doorway, at
or near the base. Carved structural members of the houses, posts,
and sometimes the beams, form another category. Finally, some poles
symbolized some special privilege. Among the Southern Kwakiutl

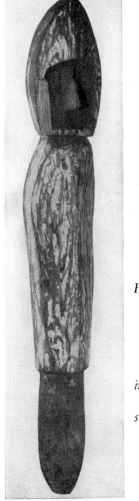

*101. Spirit canoe figure
(front and back), lower
Puget Sound. The crudity
of treatment is probably
due in part to its having
been made in a period of
decline of the native
culture under white
impact; however the art of
the Salish was at best a
simplified marginal copy of
Nootka-Kwakiutl art.*

102. Salish stone mortar carved in form of a human head; the bowl is in the top of the head. The original is in the Provincial Museum, Victoria, British Columbia.

and Nootka, the tall slender poles surmounted by a bird-like figure marked the house of the Beach-Owner—the chief who had inherited the prerogative of being the first to invite important visitors to the village to a feast. Some authorities have disagreed as to which of these types are and which are not to be considered totem poles. The only reasonable solution is that *all* are, since they all consist of symbols which belonged to a particular lineage or family and referred to events in the lineage tradition giving the right to display such a symbol, and which could be displayed by the head of that lineage. Of course the crests used on either a memorial or mortuary pole were part of the lineage property, which both the deceased chief and his successor (who had the pole carved and set up) were entitled to use. The only variation to this consistent lineage-right pattern was a specialized type of Haida pole associated with house building that sometimes included crests of both husband's and wife's lineages (Figs. 103, 104).

It was stated above that the crests displayed on totem poles and elsewhere represented encounters by clan or lineage ancestors with supernatural beings. In its broadest terms, the phrasing should have been that the crests represented important events in the family history, for the Indians believed the legendary encounters with spirits and monsters to have been actual historical events. By accepting the native viewpoint, we can account for two specialized types of carvings, used chiefly by Southern Tlingit and Kaigani Haida. In one

103. Some poles and houses at the Haida village of Skidegate (taken by the noted British Columbia photographer Maynard about 1885).

104. Haida "totem" and mortuary poles on Anthony Island, southern end of the Queen Charlotte Islands.

of these, figures of white men and European sailing vessels were carved. On one famous pole in the Alaskan Haida village of Old Kasaan, several personages who obviously represent nineteenth-century Russian priests are to be seen. The significance of these figures is that Chief Skowl, for whom the pole was carved and set up, was inordinately proud of the fact that he had successfully resisted the attempts of the Russian priests to convert him and his people to their faith. This he regarded as an important phase of his life, and so the figures of the priests were carved to symbolize it. In addition, according to the Indian concept, by thus publicly referring to the "defeat" of the foreign priests by the chief, they were ridiculed. This brings out another use of the totem pole: to refer to success over a rival, and in this way to humiliate him. When, after an altercation, a chief managed to humiliate another publicly, that event was important enough to be recorded either contemporaneously or on the victor's memorial pole. Under these circumstances the successful chief and his lineage had to be certain enough of their own strength to have no fear of desperate attempts at revenge by the chief and lineage whose disgrace was thus advertised.

The few old poles still standing in their original positions give an impression of great age, with their surfaces weathered to a silvery gray, and bits of moss growing here and there in cracks and crevices. It therefore comes as a surprise to many people to discover that few of the individual poles are even a hundred years old. After all, the wet climate must destroy even the durable red cedar, or at least the base of a pole set in soggy ground, in less than a century. In reaction to this really not very surprising discovery, a few persons have interpreted this to mean that the custom of carving and setting up totem poles was of recent origin, a conclusion completely incompatible with the facts. First of all, the earliest European explorers to visit the permanent (winter) villages saw various kinds of poles. Meares (1788) and Boit (1799) describe elaborately carved portal poles at the Nootka village of Clayoquot. Among other early voyagers, Marchand (1791) describes both portal and mortuary poles at the Haida village of Kiusta. In 1793 the Malaspina Expedition observed a tremendous Bear mortuary post set up at a chief's grave at Lituya Bay in Huna Tlingit territory. The second point of importance is that the most common functions of the totem pole—aside from such specialized variants as the Haida combinations of husband's and wife's crests (not well understood by ethnologists) and the Southern Kwakiutl–Nootka Beach–Owner posts—are related to mortuary rites and/or memorials to the dead. It has been demonstrated that the northern Northwest Coast is only part of a larger area of distribution in which some kind of pole or post, painted, plain, or with attached ornaments, was erected at or near a grave in memory of and in honor of the dead. This practice prevailed over a wide area in northeastern Siberia, among the Western Eskimo in Alaska, and southward through the interior of northwest North America at least as far south as the Columbia Basin, where we have archaeological records of cedar posts set up at the head of prehistoric graves. On the coast this widespread ancient custom was elaborated until, long before first European contacts, the totem-pole complex was evolved.

NINE

SUBAREAS AND CULTURAL RELATIONSHIPS

THE FOREGOING pages have summarized, in a very condensed fashion, the salient features of the culture area that fringed the Pacific Coast of North America from Yakutat Bay to Trinidad Bay. The aim thus far has been to point out the principal patterns that distinguished the areal civilization and combined to set it off as an entity distinct from other aboriginal American cultures. We have discussed most of the outstanding patterns: emphasis on woodworking; rectangular plank houses; specialized varieties of dugout canoes and emphasis on water transportation; untailored (wrap-around or slipover) garments principally of plant fiber; barefootedness; an economy built around fishing, with an elaborate series of types of fish traps, angling devices, and harpoons; sea-mammal hunting, important both as food source and for prestige; relatively slight use of vegetal foods; lineage–local group basic sociological unit; rank-wealth correlation defining status, and emphasis on individual status in social affairs; slavery; elaboration of ceremonialism (potlatch, dancing societies, wealth displays); and First Salmon and related types of ceremonies deriving from belief in immortality of game. At the same time, our hasty survey has touched on local variations of these primary patterns and specialized local developments. It will be worthwhile to review these traits and complexes of limited distribution, to define the subareas, or provinces, within the Northwest Coast area, to determine the inferences to be gleaned from indications of relationships between these subdivisions and between them and the neighboring culture areas.

Beginning in the north, it is fairly clear that the Tlingit, Haida, the Tsimshian formed a sub-unit, or province, of areal culture, in which the northern divisions of the Kwakiutl, particularly the Haisla, participated in a marginal fashion—that is, these latter peoples shared some, but not all, of the distinctive traits. Some of the chief features of this Northern Province were:

"Joined" house construction (plates slotted to receive planking)
Rod-and-slat armor (rod armor in northwest California also)
Porcupine-quill embroidery (infrequent)
"Elbow" adze
One-piece barbed harpoon points
Hafted stone mauls (also Heiltsuk and Bella Coola)
V-shaped halibut hook
Woman's labret (also Haisla and Heiltsuk)
Man's breechclout
Leggings (ceremonial)
Blankets in twilled twining (if true that Tsimshian formerly wove articles of "Chilkat blanket" technique)
Tobacco chewing with lime
Matrilineal social organization with crests (also Haisla; Bella Bella in imperfect form)
Crest displays principal ceremonial
Cremation (Haida only rarely)
Highly stylized representative art (also Haisla and Heiltsuk)

Several of these traits immediately suggest Eskimo-Aleut parallels: the elbow adze, the hafted stone maul, one-piece barbed harpoon heads (non-toggling), labrets (although the form varied), and rod-and-slat armor. When we add to this list a few sporadic but specific items such as Aleut-style atlatls (with unmistakable Tlingit carved decoration) collected at Cross Sound by the explorer Vancouver, the umiak seen by La Pérouse at Lituya Bay, and the occurrence of sinew-backed and compound bows among the Tlingit, the existence of Eskimo-Aleut influence cannot be overlooked. It is of no great consequence whether the material objects were captured in Tlingit raids or acquired through trade. There has been a tendency on the part of some students to attribute all Northwest Coast–Eskimo

(and Aleut) parallels as representing cultural borrowings by the latter groups, but it is more reasonable to assume that the interchange
flowed in both directions.

Another line of influence in the Northern Province is indicated
by such items as the man's breechclout, leggings, the occasional use
of porcupine-quill embroidery, sinew-backed bows, bows with string
guard, and cremation, all of which point to the Athapascans of the
interior as their source. We know that certain Tlingit and Tsimshian
groups—the Chilkat, the Stikine, and the Niska particularly—carried
on considerable trade with the interior people, and were in a position
to acquire not only furs and placer copper, but manufactured objects
and techniques as well. Although it is often assumed that the matrilineal organization of the Athapascans of the interior (Ten'a, Tanaina,
Atna, Loucheux, Tsetsaut, Tahltan, Western Nahane, Babine, Chil-
cotin, Carrier), and of the Eyak, represented coastal influence, the
opposite may be true.

Southward, the next province to set itself apart is that of the
Wakashan-speaking (Kwakiutl and Nootka) groups. The isolated
northernmost Salish, the Bella Coola, belong with this subarea culturally, at least on the basis of data from the early historic and
ethnographic horizons, although they retained a few traits reminiscent of the patterns of their southern kinsmen. Some of the unique
traits and complexes of this cultural subdivision are:

"D" adze (adjacent Coast Salish also)
Curved halibut hook (adjacent Coast Salish also)
End-thrown sealing harpoons with finger rests or finger holes
Sealskin floats for sea-mammal hunting
Harpoon rest on canoe
Whaling with lines and floats (Nootka only)
Ritual use of human corpses and skeletons
Lineage–local group organization with bilateral bias
Dancing societies (borrowed in Northern Province, and correlated
    with crests; borrowed by Salish to some extent)
Movable masks, puppets and similar mechanical devices in ritual

Despite the geographical distance separating the two regions,
this list includes a lengthier series of features reminiscent of Eskimo-
Aleut culture than the preceding. As Boas pointed out long ago, the
end-thrown sealing harpoon with finger rests or finger holes is very
probably a form related to the use of the atlatl. The use of sealskin

floats, the harpoon rest, the whole Nootkan whaling complex, the ritual use of human remains, and the use of mechanically operated masks and puppets and the like are all Eskimo-Aleut traits, and some of them, like whaling, are demonstrably old in Eskimo culture, according to archaeological evidence. We may note, too, that for the most part these traits are of a different order from the Eskimo-Aleut elements of the Northern Province. Anyone might find a hafted stone maul, or an umiak, at an abandoned or massacred Eskimo camp, and, impressed by the object's obvious practicality, take it home to use and eventually even copy it. However, the complicated techniques and rituals of the whaling complex are obviously of a different order. They could only be learned and adopted after a long period of intimate contact. This is even more understandable when one considers that the whaling rituals were jealously guarded secrets among both the Nootka and the Eskimo. Another point of interest, although its significance is not entirely clear, is that the Nootka actually practiced two different kinds of whaling: one, actual whale hunting with harpoons and floats, identical in technique to that of the Eskimo of Bering Sea and parts of the Arctic coasts, and second, a ritual procedure corresponding closely to that associated with the lance hunting of Aleut. The absence of the whaling complex among most of the Kwakiutl (except for certain groups in Quatsino Sound) can only be attributed to its abandonment, because it is inconceivable that these people, so closely related culturally and linguistically to the Nootka, should not have practiced this art at one time. Furthermore, it is precisely the Kwakiutl who have retained the Eskimo-type harpoon rest on their hunting canoes. They also used sealskin and seal-bladder floats when harpooning smaller sea mammals. Human remains played a part in magical rituals as well as in certain of their dancing society performances. In brief, then, we have a very definite indication that the Nootka, and undoubtedly their Kwakiutl relatives also, were at one time in close contact with people who participated in a considerable number of Eskimo and Aleut activities. The absence of these particular Eskimoid complexes among the Tlingit, Haida, and Tsimshian suggests that these last-named three nations may have intruded on and disrupted a former very active route of communication and cultural influence. It is also interesting to note that there are no cultural features distinctive of the Wakashan province that suggests influences from the adjacent interior, with the unimportant exception of coiled basketry. We know that the latter was introduced among some Nootka groups within historical times as a result of contact with Salish in the Fraser River canneries and the Puget Sound hop fields.

A number of complexes shared by the northern and the Wakashan provinces are not found elsewhere in the area. These include the following:

> Sporadic use of pile dwellings
> Canoe type (except Nootka)
> Suspended-warp loom (adjacent Salish also)
> Twined robe of vegetal fibers with three straight sides and curved
>   lower edge
> Urine used as detergent
> Extreme rigidity of social ranking
> Kerfed, bent, and sewn (or pegged) wooden boxes
> Pre-European use of iron (in small quantities)

The significance of the foregoing complexes varies. Construction of pile dwellings, for example, may reflect both superior engineering skill and the fact that in the rugged terrain of the northern coasts, extensive areas suitable for habitation were scarce. The type of loom and the form of robe woven on it apparently represented the basic pattern from which the highly specialized Chilkat blanket was developed. A number of Salish neighbors of the Kwakiutl and Nootka are reported to have made the kerfed and bent boxes. In all probability, however, most of the boxes of this type that they possessed— like most of their Nootka-style canoes—were articles received in trade. The use of urine as a detergent, especially in view of its ceremonial associations, is unquestionably related to Eskimo-Aleut practices. The pre-European use of iron points in the same direction, although rather than representing diffusion of a cultural concept, it indicates trade connections with Asia through Eskimo and Aleut. Iron, in small quantities, used for cutting tools first appears in Eskimo culture in the horizon designated "Punuk," after the St. Lawrence Island site where it was first identified, dated at about 1000 A.D. The iron tools that the first European explorers like Captain Cook observed on the Northwest Coast, and the obvious familiarity with the material that led to its demand by the natives in exchange for their furs, mean that the trade connections continued up to the historic period. The significance of established trade channels is that such contacts between peoples facilitate transmission of culture traits along with or in addition to the material objects bartered.

Adjoining the Wakashan province on the east and south, we find that the Coast Salish, the Chinook, and the small enclaves of miscellaneous linguistic affiliation such as the Quileute-Chemakum, probably the Klatskanie, and the small tribelets of the central Oregon coast, formed a subdivision by virtue of sharing a series of distinctive modifications of general Northwest Coast pattern. Not all of the provincially distinctive traits were shared by all of the groups, but there is a sufficiently high degree of correlation to link them all together. The Salish-Chinook province is distinguished by the following:

Mat-lodge temporary dwellings
Coiled basketry (recent among some Nootka)
Woman's basketry cap (truncated conical form)
Dog-wool blankets and the double-bar loom (Gulf of Georgia and
    Straits of Juan de Fuca only)
Closely twined wool blankets ("nobility blankets")
Chinook-type head deformation
Loosely defined system of social rank
Spirit-canoe ceremony
Guardian spirit singing
Abbreviated version of Nootka dancing society, with dog-eating
Small steam sweatlodge

Most of the items in the foregoing list are obviously interior traits and complexes. The fact that there are so many may reasonably be interpreted to indicate that the Coast Salish and perhaps the Chinook retained a great deal of their ancient cultural heritage after they entered the coastal region. The mat lodge that they used as a temporary shelter at fishing camps and the like, was, of course, one of the very common house types east of the Cascades. Steam sweating has an extensive inland distribution. Coiled basketry, again, was widespread in the Plateau region, and extended through the Great Basin into central California. The type of woman's basketry cap had a widespread distribution in the Plateau. Even though the dog-hair blanket and the double-bar loom on which it was woven had a limited distribution in the province, it appears to be a significant feature, because the blanket itself was woven in the same checkerwork technique as the rabbitskin robe so common throughout the Plateau and the Great Basin. It is even possible, as was suggested in an interesting paper published some years ago, that this Salish weaving complex may ultimately be derived via the Plains and Southwest from a Mesoamerican center of origin, presumably with the rabbitskin robe as the connecting link.

Both the loosely organized social structure that conforms only superficially to the basic Northwest Coast pattern of graded social status and the comparatively simple and unelaborate ceremonial patterns, are reminiscent of Plateau and Great Basin cultures. Here, of course, appraisals must be made on the basis of degree rather than presence or absence of specific concrete elements, but nonetheless, it seems quite clear that insofar as Salish-Chinook society and ritualism vary from coastal standards of rigidity and elaboration, they resemble patterns more at home east of the Cascades. Incidentally, it is worth noting that the heritage, or borrowing, of interior features in almost every instance indicates linkages with the Interior Salish and Sahaptin groups, and in this respect differs from the suggestions of interior influence on the three northernmost nations whose cultural ties appear to be with the Northern Athapascan divisions.

There are very few traits and complexes peculiar to this culture province and that of the Wakashan-speaking peoples aside from those attributable to distribution of material objects through trade, such as canoes and wooden boxes made by Nootka and Kwakiutl, and Nootkan hats, and a few complexes like Nootkan whaling with all its ritual accompaniments and certain ceremonial patterns. The principal inter-province parallel is one connected with house construction, in which the framework of the house was structurally separate from the horizontal removable planking of the walls. It appears to have been only the Coast Salish and Chemakum-Quileute in their areal subdivisions who used this type of structure. The Chinook and the central Oregon coast groups apparently did not.

The potlatch is the principal complex shared by all three provinces just described, but lacking in the remainder of the area.

Northwestern California, that is to say, the focus of culture along the lower Klamath, together with the culturally marginal Athapascan groups of southwest Oregon and the adjoining northwest corner of California, formed the fourth distinctive subdivision of Northwest Coast culture. While we have seen that basically Northwest Coast patterns underlie the civilization of the lower Klamath, the developments there were in many respects the most aberrant of the entire area. Some specific traits patently reflect central California influences. Others are more difficult to identify as to source. We may list the outstanding distinctive features:

Men's house–sweathouse complex with direct fire sweating
Wooden pillow and stool
Plank dwelling with three-pitch roof and central pit
Specialized canoe type
Woman's basketry cap
Straight adze
Grinding and leaching of acorns
Featherwork decoration (woodpecker scalps, etc.)
Wealth-display ceremonials and World Renewal rites

The first two items mentioned as regional peculiarities have a most remarkable distribution, the significance of which cannot be interpreted at present. The entire complex associated with the construction of a large sweathouse, direct fire sweating, draft-exit tunnel, and use as a men's house is strongly reminiscent of the Western Eskimo *kashim*. The complex likewise has a number of similarities to the Southwestern *kiva*. It is impossible to determine as yet whether or not these three institutions actually have any genetic relationship.

The second item—the use of wooden pillows and stools—is again reminiscent of Eskimo culture, although the specific forms are not identical. If more regional elements had an identical distribution, we might be justified in regarding them as representing tag ends, as it were, of influence from the north. The canoe type characteristic of this province seems to be the local elaboration of the so-called "shovelnose canoe," widely, if sporadically, distributed over the coastal area wherever river travel was frequent. The type of woman's basketry cap, the entire acorn complex and its economic importance, featherwork decoration, tobacco smoking in the tubular pipe were all widespread in aboriginal central California.

Our hurried analysis of regional specializations within the Northwest Coast area has emphasized the fact that four fairly clearly defined provinces existed—three of these, it appears, reveal cultural relationships of at least moderate strength with the non-coastal cultures of the adjacent regions. The Northern Province also shows traces of superficial influence from southwestern Alaska. At first glance this situation is not particularly noteworthy; after all, it is what one normally expects to find. People acquire new traits and complexes from groups with whom they have the most contact. The principal significance arises in the first place from the fact that the Wakashan subarea has been demonstrated to have few or no traces of direct interior influence, and second, it includes a series of features that very strongly suggest close cultural linkages to Eskimo-Aleut, from whom the groups in this area are now separated by several hundreds of miles and a number of alien nations. The most logical inference to be drawn from this situation is that the earliest inhabitants of the northern coasts—the people with whom the ancestors of the modern Kwakiutl and Nootka came into contact (or who may have been the ancestors of the Kwakiutl and Nootka)—possessed a culture, if not specifically Eskimo, at least Eskimoid in its essential features. Theirs must have been the southernmost extension of the highly specialized and ancient circumpolar tradition. That is, the ancestral culture of the Northwest Coast, whether it was specifically "Eskimo" with all the cultural and ethnic connotations of the term, or, as may have been the case, was a slightly watered-down derived version, nonetheless was based on the essential patterns of ancient Western Eskimo civilization: it was a culture oriented toward the sea, with an emphasis on navigation and the hunting of sea mammals, and a tradition of neat craftsmanship in working wood and bone. The recent discoveries of an archaeologically early pattern in the lower Fraser region that is distinguished from the successive later levels precisely by possession of articles definitely Eskimo in type, such as one-piece toggling harpoon heads, bone foreshafts, an abundance of ground slate implements, as well as definitely Eskimo-type labrets, seems to corroborate this hypothesis. If the Eskimoid type of the original Northwest Coast culture is eventually proved, it will go a long way toward explaining the uniqueness of the Northwest Coast in relation to aboriginal cultures of ethnographic times in western North America.

An older interpretation of Northwest Coast culture as essentially an extension of that of northeast Asia, contacts with which were disrupted by "the intrusion of the Eskimo into western Alaska" no longer can be sustained. Investigations of recent years in Eskimo and Aleut archaeology demonstrate that those people have occupied the shores of Bering Strait, southwest Alaska, and the Aleutian Islands continuously since before the birth of Christ. The Asiatic influences that reached the Northwest Coast must have been transmitted by Eskimo and Aleut, or else formed a part of the ancestral sea-hunting culture. In fine, all the light of modern evidence fits the hypothesis that the source of the Northwest Coast civilization, as we know it from modern ethnography, was a derivation of that of the ancient Eskimo. Those old patterns were modified and adapted to the richer and milder environment in the course of time, and further modified, and eventually enriched and elaborated to new heights by the ancestors of the Tlingit, Haida, and Tsimshian, and Salishan-speaking peoples as well, who worked their way down to the coast from the interior.

BIBLIOGRAPHY

The literature on the aboriginal cultures of the Northwest Coast is both abundant and widely scattered. For convenience of reference, it may be broken down into two principal categories: early historic accounts, that is, descriptions of natives made by early explorers and fur traders; the second, recent studies made by ethnologists. The early records, although for the most part limited to observations (since with rare exceptions the writers could not converse with the natives at any length but reported only what they could see), are often lively and vivid. The recent descriptions, based on questioning Indian informants about customs, many of which have been discarded and must be reconstructed from memory, are more complete, but lack the vitality of firsthand observations. Some of the best-known and more accessible of the early historic accounts are:

Cook, James, and James King, *A voyage to the Pacific Ocean, undertaken by the command of His Majesty, for making discoveries in the Northern Hemisphere . . . in the years 1776 to 1780.* 3 vols. Various editions.
    First description of the Nootka.
Dixon, George, *A voyage round the world, but more particularly to the North-West Coast of America; performed in 1785–1788, in the "King George" and "Queen Charlotte,"* [by] *Captain Portlock and Dixon,* London, 1789.
    First description of the Haida.
Howay, F. W. (ed.), *Voyages of the "Columbia" to the Northwest Coast 1787–1790 and 1790–1793,* Massachusetts Historical Society, Collections, Boston, Massachusetts, vol. 79, 1941.
Jewitt, John R., *A narrative of the adventures and sufferings of John R. Jewitt; . . . during a captivity of nearly three years among the Savages of Nootka Sound; with an account of the manners, mode of living, and religious opinions of the natives.* Many editions. Middletown, Connecticut, 1815.
    A very detailed description of native life, and livelier reading than many novels!
Mackenzie, Alexander, *Voyages from Montreal, on the River St. Lawrence through the Continent of North America, to the Frozen and Pacific Oceans; in the years 1789 and 1793. With a preliminary account of the rise, progress, and present state of the fur trade of that country,* London, 1801.
    Mackenzie crossed the Rockies and the Cascades in 1793, coming down the Bella Coola River. His is the first detailed description of the Bella Coola, although Vancouver had surveyed Dean and Burke channels the same year.

Meares, John, *Voyages made in the years 1788 and 1789, from China to the North West Coast of America, to which are prefixed an introductory narrative of a voyage performed in 1786, from Bengal, in the ship Nootka; Observations on the probable existence of a North West passage, etc.,* 2 vols., London, 1791.

Vancouver, George, *A voyage of discovery to the North Pacific ocean and round the world, performed in the years 1790–1795,* 3 vols. Various editions.

Descriptions of Nootka, and brief descriptions of various other groups: Coast Salish, Kwakiutl, etc.

Aside from a few works on Northwest Coast art style, two of which are cited below, there are no general popular works on the area, nor, strange to say, is there anything like the number of popular books describing the cultures of the individual groups such as there are on tribes of the Plains or the Southwest. The principal honorable exception to this statement is found in a series of brief but good descriptive accounts prepared for school use by the Department of Education of British Columbia (Victoria, B.C.): the "British Columbia Heritage Series: Our Native Peoples" (vol. 1, Introduction to our Native Peoples; vol. 2, Coast Salish; vol. 4, Haida; vol. 5, Nootka; vol. 6, Tsimshian; vol. 7, Kwakiutl; vol. 10, Bella Coola [other volumes in the series treat of groups of the interior]). There is a very extensive professional literature in anthropological journals and series, but even there most of the works deal with some particular trait or complex—houses, weaving, potlatches, and the like; there are relatively few reasonably complete descriptions of any single native nation. A list of books and monographs, most of which should be available in any large public library, follows:

Boas, Franz, The social organization and secret societies of the Kwakiutl Indians, based on personal observations and on notes made by George Hunt, *U.S. National Museum Report for 1895*, Washington, D.C., 1897.

Davis, Robert Taylor, William Reagh, and Alvin Lustig, Native Arts of the Pacific Northwest, *Stanford Art Series*, Stanford, California, 1949.

Drucker, Philip, The Northern and Central Nootkan Tribes, *Bureau of American Ethnology*, Bulletin 144, Washington, D.C., 1951.

Garfield, Viola E., Tsimshian Clan and Society, *University of Washington Publications in Anthropology*, vol. 7, no. 3, Seattle, Washington, 1939.

Gunther, Erna, Klallam ethnography, *University of Washington Publications in Anthropology*, vol. 1, no. 5, Seattle, Washington, 1927.

Halliday, William, *Potlatch and totem*, Toronto, 1935.

An interesting but somewhat administratively slanted account by a man who was Indian Agent for the Southern Kwakiutl for many years.

Hill-Tout, Charles, *British North America: The Far West. The Home of the Salish and Déné*, London, 1907.

Inverarity, Robert Bruce, *Art of the Northwest Coast Indians*, Berkeley and Los Angeles, California, 1950.

Kroeber, A. L., Handbook of the Indians of California, *Bureau of American Ethnology*, Bulletin 78, Washington, D.C., 1925. (Chapters on Yurok, Karok, and Hupa Indians.)

McIlwraith, T. F., *The Bella Coola Indians*. 2 vols., Toronto, 1948.

Niblack, Albert P., The Coast Indians of southern Alaska and northern British Columbia, *U.S. National Museum Report for 1888*, pp. 225–386, Washington, D.C., 1890.

Olson, Ronald L., The Quinault Indians, *University of Washington Publications in Anthropology*, vol. 6, no. 1, Seattle, Washington, 1936.

Ray, Verne F., Lower Chinook ethnographic notes, *University of Washington Publications in Anthropology*, vol. 7, no. 2, Seattle, Washington, 1938.

Smith, Marion W., The Puyallup-Nisqually, *Columbia University Contributions to Anthropology*, vol. 32, New York, 1940.

Swan, James G., *The Northwest Coast, or Three Years' Residence in Washington Territory*, New York, 1857.

For those interested in ethnological monographs, many, on individual tribes, will be found in the following institutional series:

American Museum of Natural History, especially in the Memoirs series, reporting the results of the Jesup North Pacific Expedition (chiefly on Tlingit, Haida, and Southern Kwakiutl).

Bureau of American Ethnology (on Tlingit, Tsimshian, Southern Kwakiutl, Nootka, northwestern California groups).

University of California (northwestern California groups, Coast Salish, Northern Kwakiutl [Haisla and Wikeno]).

University of Washington (Coast Salish, Chinook, Nootka [Makah]).

National Museum of Canada (Tsimshian).

Most monographs in the foregoing series give bibliographies in which additional references may be found. In addition, a very useful compendium, the *Ethnographic Bibliography of North America*, by G. P. Murdock (second edition), Human Relations Area File, New Haven, Connecticut, 1953, lists a great many books, short papers, etc., on the areal cultures.

INDEX

PHILIP DRUCKER is one of the leading anthropologists in this country and an authority on the aboriginal cultures of the American Northwest. He was born on January 13, 1911, in Chicago, Illinois, and was educated at the University of California where he received his doctorate in anthropology in 1936. Since 1940 he has been a staff anthropologist with the Bureau of American Ethnology of the Smithsonian Institution.

Dr. Drucker has done field-work on the Northwest Coast since 1933, made an ethnographic study of the Nootka Indians in 1935 as a Social Science Research Council predoctoral fellow, and an ethnographic survey of the Northwest Coast for the University of California program in "Culture Element Distribution" in 1936. As National Research Council postdoctoral fellow in 1938, he made an archaeological survey of the Northwest Coast. He has also made archaeological investigations in southern Mexico. His most recent work has been a study of the cultural adaptation and acculturation among Indians of the Northwest Coast.

Dr. Drucker is the author of many anthropological studies, among them *Rank, Wealth, and Kinship in Northwest Coast Society* (1939), *Archeological Survey of the Northern Northwest Coast* (1943), and *The Northern and Central Nootkan Tribes* (1951).